Up In The Holler

Memories of a
Coal Camp Kid

By Darrell E. Wilcox

With Annette Savage Williams

First printing.

A Williams Savage Books Publication

Williams Savage Books
P.O. Box 3724
Ramona, CA 92065

Email: WilliamsSavageBooks@aol.com

www.WilliamsSavageBooks.com

Dedication

This book is dedicated to my mother,
Carrie Gillen Wilcox

Up In The Holler

Memories of a
Coal Camp Kid

Table of Contents

Introduction

It has been said that getting started on a project is usually the hardest part. I would be the first person to agree, having started this book and stopped more times than I can remember. I am sitting down to put pen to paper once more, and this time I am determined to tell my story.

Over the many years I have been on this earth it is hard to recall all the people who have said, "Darrell, you've lived such an interesting life! You should write a book about all you've seen and lived through."

The world today is such a different place from when I was growing up. In just two or three generations we have literally come from the horse-and-buggy era to being able to buy a ticket to ride on a rocket to outer space.

For most kids today, their grandfathers or great-grandfathers never used the Internet or knew what an iPod was. They would never believe what I went through as a child. I want to tell young people that we only have a certain number of days on this earth. Do not take anything for granted, make the most of the opportunities that you are given, and before you realize it you will be looking back and asking yourself, "Where did the time go?"

The reason I am writing this book is so I, and all who have also come from humble beginnings, will never forget where we came from and what we went through to reach this place in time and history. And I want to tell the kids growing up today that they have it good compared to the time and place where I grew up.

Part 1

WYCO, WEST VIRGINIA

Chapter 1

Wyco Holler

My story begins when I was born in the Wyco holler coal camp on December 28, 1931.

Wyco, West Virginia, is located in Wyoming County, in the Slab Fork district. It's an area that had many large trees and bushes.

When folks from home talk about our town, they call it "Wyco holler," but its name is just Wyco. Nobody is exactly sure where the name came from. Maybe it was named after Wyoming County, or maybe after the coal mine, the Wyoming Coal Company. Wyco is about a mile from the Raleigh County line, which was sometimes marked Ral-Co on one side of the map and Wy-Co on the other, so maybe that's how it got its name.

"Holler" means "a hollow place or valley." It's a word that's been around since the mid-1800s. Wyco, at an elevation of 1,545 feet, is mountain country, and the hollers are large and deep.

There were no roads in the mountains, so you had to walk or ride a horse. Since we didn't have any horses, we mostly walked everywhere we went — that was just the way we lived.

In the 1930s and '40s, the Wyco holler coal camp was a productive coal mining community with homes and schools, but no hospital and only one doctor.

There was a single store where miners' families bought their goods with scrip earned by the head of the household and older sons who still lived at home.

Miners' union strikes were common, and life became very difficult when that happened.

The town also had a pool hall, a place where men worked out their frustrations by drinking or fighting — my dad could be found doing both.

Mining was our way of life. It was what we knew. The mines were about the only place a man could earn a living that didn't require him to have finished school, which was true for my dad.

As I think about growing up in those days, I am sure people today would say we had a very dysfunctional family in a very poor community. But we didn't know anything different and I didn't have any other families outside the holler to compare to, so this was what we knew as normal. I really believed everyone lived and worked this way. But once I left the holler, my eyes were sure opened!

The Wilcox Family

My father's name was Walter Wilcox, but everyone called him by his nickname, Red, because he had red hair. My mother was Carrie (Gillen) Wilcox.

There were quite a few uncles and aunts. On the Gillen side, there were Marie, Tom, Ann and Bet. On the Wilcox side, there were Charlie, Buster and Liz Bell.

The Wilcox and Gillen families were all born and raised in Damascus, Virginia. I don't know very much about my father and mother's life because they didn't talk about it, and I never knew of any family pictures that were taken back then.

My father was eleven years old when his father died. Because he was the oldest boy in the family, he quit school and had to go to work to help support them. I don't know what he did to work at that young age, but he worked.

When he married my mom, they moved to Wyco where he worked in the coal mines. They moved to Wyco because he knew that was one of the few places he could go to make some good money, which he needed to do once he had a wife.

My mother was a very small woman with a great sense of humor, and she was very hardworking. She had all her kids at home as there were no hospitals. The women in the coal camp helped each other when they gave birth. If you had seen how small my mother was, you wouldn't believe that she could have fourteen kids who lived — eight boys and six girls — along with two miscarriages.

I have no idea why they had so many, maybe there just wasn't any way to protect against getting pregnant or they didn't know enough to stop — God only knows.

The Wilcox kids in order of birth were Robert James, Walter Lee Jr. "Junior," Vivian Ann, Jimmy, Darrell Edward (me), Joe Dan "Jake," Carolyn Sue, Johnny Lee, Carrie Jeanette, William Harold, Drema Marie, Rena Marie, Rita Gail "Susie," and Michael Dennis.

We were all born in the same little two-bedroom house up in the holler. It was a tiny home with a small living room, kitchen and very small bedrooms. There were only four rooms in the whole house.

I'm not sure who misspelled my name as "Dearrel" on my original birth certificate, but it definitely wasn't our family doctor, Dr. Darrell Wilkinson. He knew how my name was supposed to be spelled because I was named after him. His signature on the certificate is very different from the handwriting for my name. In fact, it looks as though he filled out everything except my name, so maybe that was added later. My name was eventually spelled right on my registered certificate.

There were a lot of kids in our family, so we slept six to a bed — "three up and three down" is what we called it. Mom, Dad and my sisters slept in the other bedroom. We thought that was the way everyone lived.

I spent most of my childhood in that house. Until I was nineteen years old, it was my home. There was no running water or indoor plumbing. We had an outhouse as a toilet and used magazines for toilet paper, or you just went on the ground if you were in the mountains and used leaves. That was how it was for everyone in the holler.

All the houses were mostly the same, either two or three bedrooms, and all the same color, white with black trim. As far as I know and can remember, the water we had mostly came from a spring.

We barely survived, and I left as soon as I could — as soon as I got a chance. I never missed that way of life because there was nothing to hope for except working in the coal mines.

Family Dynamics

My mother never got anything but hard work. I believe the reason she was pregnant all the time was alcohol, because Dad was always drunk and couldn't keep his hands off of her.

All my sisters were good to help Mom with the house-keeping and watching the younger kids, and we all had chores to do every day.

The way we lived back then was difficult, I have to say.

Father was the boss. He was a hard worker, and when he came home from work he told us what he wanted us to do, and we didn't dare say no. When he said to do something, we did it!

If my mother said, "When your dad comes home, I am going to tell him what you did," we obeyed her right away! We knew what he would do to us and we didn't want any of that!

We were scared when he came home because we knew that we were going to get it if everything wasn't done to his satisfaction. We always had the garden hoed in the morning. If you heard Dad holler one time, it meant you had to build a fire with wood and coal in the Burnside stove (a potbellied stove) in the kitchen. In the wintertime, we used coal, but it would go out during the night. When you reached twelve years old, you were the one that got up in the morning and built the fire. When Dad yelled your name, it was your turn until one of the others reached a certain age, then that kid built the fire. Dad only yelled our name one time — he didn't have to yell twice.

If some of the kids today saw how we lived, it would scare them pretty bad, and probably some grown people, too. But we thought everybody lived like that.

Today, people just turn their heater or cooler on; back then, you had to go in the mountains and cut your wood for winter heat and for cooking. Cutting wood was one of the jobs we kids had to do.

Another way of providing fuel for the stove was to take buckets down to the mines and pick up pieces of coal that fell off the cars. We used five-gallon buckets, but if you were too small to carry the bucket, you could still pick up the coal and put it in another family member's bucket. We knew that if we didn't help, we would freeze. It sure taught us how to work.

What really kept us warm in the wintertime were the six of us kids in the same bed, with three of us lying at each end. I didn't mind because it felt good to sleep close to one another because it was so cold. But you couldn't move too much or the bigger boys would pop you one.

In the summer, things would change. Then, we might sleep in the bed, on the porch or out on the ground. That was how everyone lived, or so we thought.

Sitting on our porch was fun, but if you fell off you were in trouble. The house was built on the side of the mountain, and it was a long way down — maybe twenty feet — and the ground was like a rock!

One of the best times in our lives was when my mother was on the front porch with us, giving us some chocolate candy she made in a black pan. The best part of being on the porch was that our dad wasn't around.

When I was younger, about grade-school age, our most peaceful time was during the week when Dad was working. I always hated to see Friday evening come because all hell broke loose — that's when my dad got mean. I think about those times even to this day. The rest of the weekend, the only time we got peace was if Dad had to go somewhere. Every Saturday morning, he found things for us to do, then he left and went to the pool hall or to town somehow and get a bottle. When he left, we were tickled to death because it was so nice and quiet.

He was mean when he got drunk, which was usually at night. If we heard him coming, we hurried to bed or stayed out of the house until he went to sleep. On weekends when Dad was drunk, we waited and wouldn't go to bed until he got home and went to sleep. Only then did we know where it was safe to sleep. We were glad when he came home and went straight to bed.

On weekends, a lot of bad things happened when he got his booze and came home drunk and mean. It was hell. When my two older brothers got bigger, they tried to control him and protect the rest of the kids from his meanness. They could take him on, but he still carried a big knife.

No matter the weather, if it was snowing, raining or blazing hot, when dad came home drunk, he was mean. Maybe it was because he was hit over the head with a pool stick or maybe it was just the alcohol, but he was mean to us.

Since Dad went to work at such a young age, maybe he was depressed from not having much of a childhood. But he was never too depressed not to beat the hell out of us.

As long as dad was gone or in bed, we were okay. We just tried to stay out of his way.

Bill Davenport is the one who hit Dad with the pool cue. Dad was a big old red-headed guy. He beat Bill in a game of pool, and Bill was mad. While Dad was sitting on a high pool chair, he came at him and hit him with the big end of the stick. They had to take Dad 28 miles out of the holler to the hospital in Beckley with the help of one of his best friends, Les Carpenter, a little skinny guy.

When the ambulance guy said, "This guy is dead, turn around and go to the funeral home," Les threatened to shoot both ambulance drivers if they didn't take him to the hospital. Dad didn't get out of the hospital until nine months later. He was lucky to survive. But when he came out, he was still meaner than hell.

I remember when we were little, my dad would run us out into the snow barefooted just for meanness. We had to stand in the snow on one foot at a time and try to keep our feet from freezing until Dad went to sleep and we could come back in the house.

When the older brothers got big, they had their fights with Dad. He had no trouble fighting with his own boys, even cutting my brother Junior with a knife.

It was on a Friday night when all the miners were in the beer joint that Dad cut him so bad it took ninety stitches in his stomach to sew him up. When he came home that night, my brothers fought with Dad again, and Junior busted all the stitches loose. There was blood all over the kitchen. I don't remember how he lived to get to the doctor, but he lived.

This went on until I started working in the coal mine and got big enough to stop him. I remember it was a Friday morning and we were getting ready to go to work in the mines when I told him right in front of my mother, "If you come home tonight raising hell with Mom and the kids, I am personally going to whip your butt."

And he knew I would do it, too. That's all it took. He knew that we would have it out with him if he came home drunk and tried to start something.

Life back then was nothing like today. When you need help nowadays, you can call the police. Then, we had no one but ourselves to protect us when we were growing up.

That is the way we lived in the coal camp.

Chapter 2

Life in the Holler

The coal mine was up the holler and was the center of our life and livelihood.

Living in the holler was mostly routine, day in and day out. Most families lived the way we did, in little houses with outdoor toilets.

The mountains surrounded the holler, and the houses were built on the sides of the mountain near the bottom, but never right on the bottom. No way would anyone build a house on the very bottom because when the thunderstorms and snow came, you would be flooded out.

Kids in the mining camp were only allowed to play where the houses were or up in the mountains. We couldn't go around the mine or the miners because their work was very dangerous. We were strictly taught to stay clear of that area except on the weekends when the miners weren't working. That was a treat because we could use a real bathroom and the miners' shower room, all less than a mile from the house.

When we were small, our moms gave us a bath in the washtub at home on the weekends, if they had time, or we washed in the river when the weather was warm. When we got older, we went to the miners' bathroom and showered. We washed up with homemade soap.

Being such a hard worker, Dad always had something going on, even on the weekends. He also made us work with him if he needed us, and the girls would do things around the house when they got big enough. Everyone worked hard — that's the way we lived and survived. Today, if you tell people all that we had to do, they look at you like you're crazy.

People might think it was crazy the way we lived, but that's the way we were raised. Most families we knew functioned the same way. We respected our elders and called them Mr. or Mrs., never by their first names. And you knew better than to smoke around them because one of them would knock the cigarette right out of your mouth. If they told us what to do — and they only had to tell us once — we did it, because we knew what we would get if we didn't.

Today, I hear people say, "My child just won't mind me." That's because the parents don't let them know who is boss.

In the holler, we walked or ran wherever we needed to go. We didn't have streets or sidewalks, just dirt roads.

We also walked down the railroad tracks where the train carried the coal out of the holler and over the mountains.

The mountains were very high and steep, and there were no roads in the mountains so you had to walk or ride a horse. Since we didn't have any horses we pretty much walked everywhere we went. Sometimes we got lost in the mountains. It's a funny feeling until you find your way out.

The Smith Family

The only horses I saw belonged to two wild families that lived in two little wooden shacks high in the mountains above the camp. No one lived up there except the Smiths.

They used their horses to carry things up the mountains, but when their kids came out of the holler to go to school, they walked all the way.

I remember when one of the boys, Bill Smith, got a job in the coal mine. He would walk out of those mountains down to work every day. He worked all day in the mine, and in the evening he walked all the way back up the mountains.

Finally he bought himself a brand new car that he left at the coal camp, until one day he had a wreck — he hit a tree and was killed.

Six or eight men from the mountains came and carried his casket on their backs all the way up that mountain to their mother's house, and I went with them. I still can't believe they carried that casket by hand all the way up the mountain.

The Town

Back then, Wyco holler only had a small grocery store, a school for whites and a school for blacks, a pool hall and beer joint where the miners hung out doing lots of drinking, pool shooting and poker playing. There was nothing else to do in the holler.

The only law was in Mullens, about seven or eight miles away, so you had to protect yourself. Today we have protection, but back then we had none, so we protected ourselves and our families. You knew better than to bother someone's family; you could get killed quick and no one would ever know who did it.

Not many people stayed in Wyco long if they didn't work with the miners. They either worked or they were made to leave. It was done very quietly.

In the holler, we had no such things as police or fire departments. We took care of ourselves and we watched out for one another. Back then, if your house caught fire, you didn't have any way of saving it unless you put it out when it first started. We had open grates in the fireplaces, and you'd think with all the sparks flying around there would have been more fires. Maybe

God was with us. I saw a lot of miracles there in the holler.

Pool Hall

On the weekends, the miners went to the local pool hall, especially if they didn't have a car to drive to Mullens. They played poker or made home-brew. Miners who didn't go to the pool hall would go out by the woodshed and play cards, pitch horseshoes or shoot the breeze. There was nothing else for them to do.

A little peg-legged guy named Doug ran the pool hall. There was another building where Doug would make the best hot dogs and hamburgers. The food was great! Every now and then my mom would treat us to one. They didn't have French fries — even if we had such a thing back then there was no way to cook them. The next time you have a hot dog, put some chili on top. That is what we call a West Virginia hot dog. It is delicious!

When we boys got to be sixteen years old we were allowed in the pool hall. That was something big and we thought we were hot stuff! I saw a lot of fights there: not verbal fights — fistfights!

As soon as I turned sixteen, I started shooting pool in the pool hall. I had a great talent for it and I practiced every time I had money. Pool hustling is how I got spending money. My oldest brother helped me and let me wear his clothes so I wouldn't look too ragged. It wasn't long until I was a pretty good hustler. I loved the competition. I was like Lee Trevino was in golf. He couldn't wait to play Jack Nicklaus, and deep down Jack knew Lee was coming to challenge him. Those guys were two of the greatest golfers in the world, and real gentleman.

I made good money shooting pool, but my older brothers were careful to let me know when to leave the pool hall before the miners got so drunk they wanted to fight, because we could get hurt. It was dangerous working in the mines all week, so on the weekends the miners drank beer, shot pool and got into fights, blowing off some steam from their stressful job.

You would never see women at the pool hall and beer joint. You only saw them at the grocery store. Most of the time, women stayed home.

Entertainment

Back then, people stayed home through the week and went to one another's houses to visit on weekends. Saturday night, the Grand Ole Opry was on the radio, and we really looked forward to it. Everybody would lie down on the floor and listen to the music. I remember when Tennessee Ernie Ford sang the song, "16 Tons." That turned out to be quite a hit.

Also on the weekends, the Flaim family — Mary, Ernest, Guido and Raymond, who were Italian — played music on their front porch. We would go listen to them play their instruments, including an accordion, comb and guitar, and have a great time. It was also fun to build a fire and toast marshmallows and wieners, although not too often. That would be like going to McDonald's today. It was a treat, even if it was outside in the snow most times.

Listening to music on Saturday nights was our greatest entertainment, and it was about all there was to do in the holler until we got old enough to go to high school. A lot of us kids never got to see a movie until we went to high school.

No one had a telephone at home. It's not like today, where everyone carries a cell phone. I don't know why, but I never even thought about a telephone back then. When you lived in the holler, it was your whole world, and I guess you didn't need a phone.

Moonshiners

In Wyco, everyone knew not to go up in the mountains where the moonshine and home-brew were made. If you went there, you might not come back. It was wild up there and you could get killed. Most people in coal camp didn't want to know where moonshine was made because it was in their best interest not to know!

The revenuer went up there and they never saw him again. Most of the folks that got killed were buried in the mountains, but one of them was thrown in the river after he was killed. Pretty soon they stopped sending the Internal Revenue men back there anymore. (Revenuers were agents from the Treasury Department who were sent to enforce the laws against illegal alcohol bootlegging. Moonshiners didn't pay taxes, you see.)

The Smith brothers, from that wild family in the mountains, were moonshiners. It was so cold up there that their skin would crack.

If you dared to go up there, the Smiths wouldn't come out and greet you, but you could see someone's head peeking around the corner. If you threw a rock at the house they might come out from the bushes because they figured it was someone they knew. If you were a stranger and came up the holler, there was a good chance you would either wind up in the Guyandotte River or buried way up in the mountains.

The men also made home-brew, which is something like beer. It was made out of store-bought malt in a crock barrel and fermented ninety days. Most home-brew is dark brown in color. If you wanted to make it clear, you put light bread on top of your brew and it sucked the darkness out, making it clear.

A Kid's-Eye View

In the summertime we didn't ever wear shoes. In fact, Mom took our shoes to save them for winter. We went barefooted all the time and the bottom of our feet would get as hard as a rock. We could run as fast as deer.

In the wintertime, we usually got shoes passed down from one of the older kids. If there was a hole in the sole we used cardboard to cover it. We carried extra in our pockets to change it when we needed to, in case the cardboard got wet. When we outgrew our shoes, we gave them to the next younger kid, and he or she wore them until they were falling apart. That is what it is like being poor.

With so many kids at home there just wasn't any extra money for new clothes, especially if you were one of the younger kids. My oldest brother, Robert, used to let me wear some of his clothes. The fact is, he helped raise the family. I'm not sure we would have survived otherwise. Thank God, we had him.

Some of the people who lived in the holler thought they were too good to play with us because we were so poor and wild, but we didn't care as long as they didn't bother us. We were happy playing by ourselves.

The holler was our whole world. Growing up, I never thought about anyplace else because we really didn't know about anything outside the holler. I never learned how other people lived until I went away to barber school.

It seemed in the holler that a lot of people didn't have much hope or dreams for the future. Or maybe they didn't want to dream, so they just stayed in the coal mines. That's what most of the people did.

I had a dream when I was a little boy. When I was about six or eight years old, I used to see Mary Flaim cutting her kids' hair with hand clippers. I told myself, "I want to be a barber someday," and that dream came true.

I think if you have a dream, like me wanting to be a barber, you shouldn't let anything get in the way.

Coal Miners

The name of the coal company was Wyco Coal Company. All the coal miners in Wyco were members of the UMWA, "United Mine Workers of America" union. We never dared to say anything about John L. Lewis, the president of the union. He was like a god to the working miners. If you talked bad about him, you could get into a lot of trouble from the other men. Some people even got killed talking bad about him.

The coal mine superintendent lived in a huge house all by itself, just him and his wife. It looked like the White House. I used to do work for her, and they always treated me well. I never forgot them.

Mining was a rough life. The men worked hard through the week, drank on the weekends, played pool and poker, and then fought in the pool hall and at home.

They earned scrip, a round coin like a dollar that was worth a dollar if you spent or cashed it at the coal company-owned grocery store or the pool hall. But if you used it anywhere else, you would only get 75 cents on the dollar.

In the holler, women could draw scrip only from the store, and they could only draw as much their husbands earned working in the mine. If the money ran out, they couldn't draw any more scrip until he made more money. When they ran out of scrip, they either borrowed from their neighbor or their older sons if they were working in the mines.

I remember when my mother ran out of scrip, she would drop in on our brother Robert. If we didn't have him, I don't know what we would have done.

Life in our family seemed to get better when Robert got older. Even though he worked in the mines, he helped my mother raise us younger kids. He also protected us from our father when he came home drunk and mean.

Robert was very good to us. He was a great man, an honest man. He continued to live at home and moved to Virginia when my mom did.

When coal miners went on strike, it was bad for everybody who lived in the hollers. When things got real bad, they gave us a sack of beans, a sack of flour, and lard so you could eat biscuits, gravy, potatoes and a pot of beans or potato soup.

There's nothing like biscuits, gravy and fried potatoes. That's why we called these things "lifesavers." That was some fine food.

Miners' strikes were very bad, causing lots of fights. People had no money and they had nothing to do, so tempers would flare sometimes. They argued and many times got into fistfights with each other. It got worse the longer the strike went on.

There was a lot of drinking and fighting. Some people even got killed fighting with one another.

Just because the miners went out on strike didn't mean they closed the store, post office, beer joint or pool hall. We were thankful that the store didn't close — that would have been a disaster. We could still get a few things we needed, like a bag of potatoes or some beans.

I look back now and I can see that my dad grew those gardens and raised hogs and chickens to see us through the hard times.

Coal mining was backbreaking work. One time my father had an accident when the motor he was driving went down the slate dump. The slate dump is where they dumped the slate rock that they separated from the coal. It was up on the high mountain, very steep. I still don't know how he lived going all the way down. But somehow he made it all the way back up the holler, about two miles, walking with a broken leg.

My dad was a tough old devil. Most people who saw the spot where he came off of that mountain couldn't believe he lived through it and made it back to the coal camp by himself. But that was nothing to him; it was just the way he was. To this day I am not sure how he got to the doctor for his leg because the only hospital was a long way away in Beckley, West Virginia.

It wasn't until I went to work myself that I knew just how hard a job mining coal could be.

Segregation

The black folks lived in the holler with us. The white folks lived in the upper end of the holler above the coal camp and the black folks lived in the lower end. We all worked in the coal mines together, and truthfully, we never had any hard feelings toward one another. We worked together and then we played baseball together on the weekends.

They did have their own schools, but we kids didn't know any better because that is how it was in those days.

Everybody, blacks and whites, traded at the same store. The black miners sure did look out for me when I was working in the mine. After I finished barber school, they always complimented me for doing a good job and making it through.

We never had anyone protesting or marching up and down the streets. If anyone had a problem, I don't remember hearing about it.

We should all be able to sit down together and be friends. That is the way it should be.

Wyco Grade School

Wyco Grade School went from first grade to eighth grade, and each grade had fifteen to twenty students.

Every morning when school started, we had devotions, said the Pledge of Allegiance to the flag, and sang. We started every day of school this way. It taught me respect for God and to appreciate our country. I believe that schools today should do the same thing and it would be good for our country.

In West Virginia, you had better not say anything bad about our country. If you dared to, you'd better be prepared to duck!

When we went to school, the teacher was the boss! And if you didn't show respect, you knew what you were going to get when you got home.

They were very strict in class. On Friday evenings, if we did something bad in school that week, the principal had a big wooden paddle with five holes in it and we'd get a paddling. He made us touch our knees and then he paddled us with five hits. That really hurt! And to top it off, they told our parents, which I didn't like because my dad was mean. He gave it to us worse than we got at school.

There was no such thing as talking back to the teacher because the kids knew if they did, they would get a paddling from the teacher on Friday after school and then get it again from their dad when he got home.

Everyone respected their teachers because you knew what you were going to get if your folks found out! I sure didn't want that paddle at school and those big birch switches at home!

Back then, parents didn't go to school and say, "My kid didn't do that." People today think their kids never do anything wrong or they think it is the teacher's fault their kids act up. Kids need more discipline at home and at school, and parents need to stop thinking their kids never do anything wrong.

We had to work hard in school. We learned how to spell, do math, and all those things before we got out of grade school. We had math and spelling contests against one another. That is how they made sure we learned the material, by having us compete against one another.

At home, we never practiced reading because we didn't have any books to read. Even today, I never think about reading, but I know how to work with my hands and my mind.

When you got out of school for the day, the first place you went was home to let your mom know where you were and where you were going. There were no school buses to take you to school in the holler. We walked everywhere, and at night when we heard our mom hollering for us, that meant it was bedtime.

Chapter 3

How We Lived

Housework and Chores

Wyco women deserve all the credit in the world. They never got enough credit for what they did.

There were no carpets in those days, so on the weekends my mother scrubbed the floor. My sisters were good to help Mom around the house doing all the chores.

There were also no washing machines to wash our clothes, so Mom used the washboard with her hands and then hung them anywhere she could to let them dry. It was good for Mom that we didn't need many clothes in the summer.

When I tell people today that my mom made homemade soap they look at me like I'm crazy, but it's true. You take melted, loose, warm grease; lye; cold water; borax; and ammonia. You mix it according to the recipe and stir it up thick and white, then you pour it into a pan lined with a cloth, mark into pieces, and let it stand for two days until it becomes hard. You can add perfume to the recipe to make it smell better.

We also made other things, such as homemade butter and buttermilk, molasses, all types of bread and pastry, and more. In summer, we canned food for the winter.

Back then, you never heard anyone say they were going on a shopping trip. We only had one grocery store, and you could buy clothes, food and anything you needed there. Only people who had a car could go to Mullens, and very few people had a car.

When I was still in grade school I made money by hunting for the neighbors' cows in the mountains. There were very few cows in the holler, and I used to hunt them with my big black dog, Jigs. The cows were in those high mountains grazing and they didn't want to come out. Boy, did old Jigs bring them out. When they heard him bark, they knew he would bite their legs and they came running. My dog knew when to bite them and he knew what I wanted him to do. It was our daily routine, and it was hard.

Later, I made 75 cents a month delivering newspapers. I had to walk all the way out of the holler to the highway, which was at least two miles away. I picked up my papers and then walked all the way back to the coal camp and delivered them to the people who lived there. Many times I had to walk all that way and it would be dark and raining or snowing. Thank God, once in a while someone would drive by in a car and give me a ride. It wasn't always easy, but I did it. One thing about having to walk to the highway was that I passed where the people of the holler dumped their trash. I found a lot of pets there, like baby dogs and cats.

Family Doctor

In the holler we had only one doctor, Dr. Darrell Wilkinson, but he was only there during the week. The doctor didn't live in camp. He lived by the camp in a big, two-story house, and he deserved it. His house was by the store where the other businesses were located.

The doctor's son, Darrell Jr., was a friend of my younger brother and in the same grade at school. The Wilkinsons also had a daughter named Elizabeth.

Dr. Wilkinson made a lot of house calls and helped us in so many ways. Our family traded the doctor wood we cut in exchange for animals he got from people who didn't have money to pay their bills.

The closest hospital was 28 miles away in Beckley. One time I broke my leg and had to wait until the next day to go to the hospital. The same was true when I broke my arm. We had to wait until the next day and then find someone with a car, because we didn't have one, and then go to the hospital to get my leg and arm set. I'm sure Doctor Wilkinson looked at me, but he was a family doctor, not a specialist. He probably did as much as he could because he was very concerned with everybody in the holler.

He walked up the hills to the homes where women were having their babies and would sit and wait to help them. He always came to the house for those who were sick and the older people who were dying, sometimes waiting there until they died.

We never saw the doctor very much, but I don't know what we would have done if we didn't have him. There are not many great doctors like Doc Wilkinson. He saved a lot of our lives.

Imagine all the things that can happen to the men working in the mines. If it weren't for him, many who got injured would not have lived.

Doc was a good man. He came anytime we needed him, day or night. Can you imagine what that was like for him and his family? I have to give his wife and kids a lot of credit because that life couldn't have been easy for them, either.

I thank God we had Doc Wilkinson and his family living in the holler. There were not many doctors who would have lived in such a spot when they could have been practicing in a lot better place.

It was kind of scary living in those mountains compared to how everything is today. You couldn't just pick up the phone and call 911 and expect the paramedics to show up in five minutes, or know that a doctor or hospital is just a few blocks away. People living with all the modern conveniences today find it hard to believe how primitive our live was.

The doctor was such a nice man and good to everyone. I never heard anyone ever say anything bad about him. Wherever we saw him, either at home or at his office, he was always the same good person.

Home Remedies

Even though Dr. Wilkinson was in town, we didn't run to see him every time we got a cold, the flu or a sore throat. Mom took care of those types of things. Even today, I still use a lot of the cures mom used to treat us with when we were sick. These days, if you watch television and take everything they are trying to sell you to fix your aches and pains, you would be in a real fix.

We didn't have aspirin in those days. We used to cure aches with rubbing alcohol, one of the best medicines we had in our house. We also used it on cuts, bruises, backaches, joints and just about everything. It really works as well as all these pills people take. Just rub it on your sores or sprains, and on your joints, too. You'll be amazed what rubbing alcohol can do. I still use it instead of pills. We also used hot pads, and if we didn't have them, we used the warmth of our hands. But these days it's a lot easier to take pills instead.

Things just were not very sanitary back then. We used to use our shirttail or sleeve for a handkerchief. We used a toothbrush when we brushed our teeth — if we had one — but most of the time we used baking soda and our fingers to clean our teeth. Soda also worked for an upset stomach. If you try baking soda, not real strong, it's great for an upset stomach.

Food and Drink

On weekends, there were gardens to grow, and we had a cow, pigs and chickens to eat. We did our own butchering right in the holler.

Even though the miners worked hard Monday through Friday, in the summertime they grew gardens if we got enough rain. If we didn't get rain, then there was no garden. If the weather cooperated, we canned a lot of our food to eat in the wintertime. I thank God for the rain and for our garden!

My dad's gardens were on the mountainside. Dad made us boys work there, and when he told you it was time to hoe, you'd better have it all done or be working on it when he got home from work. You didn't stop until he said it was suppertime — only then was it okay to stop for the day.

Our father taught us all how to work, and so when we got older and went to work for someone else, we always worked hard.

In the summer when other people's gardens were ripe, we didn't think of it as stealing, we just "helped ourselves." We didn't destroy or waste anything. We took what we wanted to eat, but we sure didn't want to get caught. My old man could use that switch. The way to take chickens or other things was to do it at night or when everybody was working. It was wrong, but we didn't know any better.

We didn't have garden fruit but we picked wild fruit ourselves. Dad would wake us before daylight so we could walk up in the mountains where it was very steep to get berries. In our camp, we knew about all the different types of fruit trees and wild blackberries.

We would also pick and eat wild grapes in the woods. In winter, you wouldn't believe how sweet the grapes were. In the fall after the frost came, it made the grapes real sweet. That was a treat for us. We lived off what we found up in the mountains. We climbed right up those trees and bushes.

Henry Millam grew huge cabbage, as big as a washtub. One time my dad told Henry, "I ordered a huge pot."

Henry said, "Red, why did you order a pot so big?"

My dad said, "To cook your cabbage in on the weekend!"

We cooked almost all our food on the old cook stove that was in the kitchen, the same stove that kept us warm burning the wood we cut in the mountains or coal from the mines. There were no such things as electric or gas stoves in the holler. We never heard of barbecuing or barbecue pits, either; we just built a fire in the stove, and the flames and smoke did a great job cooking our food. Once in a while we used the oven in the store for toast, but we never did that often. In those days there were no neighborhood barbecue parties, because we just didn't do that in the holler.

Our way of life was pretty simple. It's hard to believe we didn't have much except beans, potatoes, flour, cornmeal and sugar, and the things we could make with them. We had a lot of biscuits, cornbread, fried potatoes and all types of recipes that used beans.

For breakfast, we ate biscuits, gravy and fried potatoes. For supper, it was a lot of beans or a pot of potatoes. I mentioned that we called biscuits, gravy and fried potatoes "lifesavers," because without them, many times we wouldn't have had anything to eat. And they are still fantastic! Believe me, as big as our family was, it helped save us. They were a gift from God to help us survive. To this day I don't think you can find a better breakfast. With the potatoes fried brown and crisp, there is nothing better.

The family that owned the boardinghouse where the single miners stayed was named Lookabill, and I was a friend of their son, Eddie. I never saw so much food as was on his mother's table, but I was too bashful to eat.

I was very lucky to have the Lookabills. They took me to the movies in Mullens with them on a Saturday about two or three times a year. Some of the happiest times I can remember were when I used to hunt for the cow in the mountains with my dog, and when the Lookabills took me to the movies. What a treat! A movie ticket was eleven cents, and I had five cents to spend for some candy that you can chew on for a long time. And if his parents didn't pick us up right away, we watched the movies twice.

When I got in the ninth grade, I went a lot more often, usually with Geneva Cassanelli, whose dad owned the theater.

By the time I was six years old I could milk our cows by hand. A cow has to have birthed a calf to give milk. We knew when our cows needed to be bred, but no one in our camp had a bull so we would tie a rope around our cow's neck and take it about three miles out of the holler to the only bull in the area. That was a job!

We had two cows, and it was my job to milk them until I got into high school. After that, a younger brother had to take his turn. My hands stunk from milking. I also had cow manure on my shoes, and that really stunk, too. When I went anywhere, I could smell those cows on me. It wasn't funny when I was around the girls.

From the milk, we made buttermilk by using a churn and churning by hand. The homemade butter would come to the top of the churn, and when we took it off the top, what was left was buttermilk.
We raised two or three pigs every year to have some meat, along with cows and chickens. We also raised

pigs to sell. In our world, there were no such things as horses, goats and sheep.

In November and December, all the men worked together to kill their hogs at hog killing time. It was a ritual every winter. They killed them, hung them and took all the intestines out of them. Then they got a big tub of water, built a fire under it, got it to boiling and put the hog in the hot water. When it was hot enough to skin the hog, we removed the hair from it, down to the skin.

It was quite a job! Those men all worked together when they cut up their hogs. They knew how to make bacon, ham and pork chops, and that's how we got our meat. We did the cows and chickens the same way.

The reason they killed animals in the winter was because it was freezing outside and the cold weather kept the meat from spoiling. Nobody had a refrigerator or freezer, so plain old cold weather is what we used.

We hung our meat out on our porch, way up high so no animals could get it. When we wanted some, we would go out and cut off a piece.

In the wintertime, we put all of our perishable food outside and we didn't have to worry about it spoiling. In the summertime, we bought big blocks of ice to keep the food cold.

Most of the time we used up what we butchered before the weather got hot. And when it was hot weather, we picked our chickens or skinned small animals and cooked and ate them that day so they wouldn't spoil. We did everything by the weather.

Mountain oysters are what they called the male pigs' testicles, but I didn't know what they were at first. One time we were eating supper and I kept telling my mother how good those mountain oysters were. When my dad told me what they were, I never ate them again. They were good rolled in cornmeal, but I still didn't eat them anymore.

Everything was all done by hand and it was hard work. While the hog killing was done as a group, we killed chickens and small animals ourselves. We used scalding water to pick the little feathers off our chickens, and then we cooked up some good old chicken and dumplings or fried chicken and gravy. That was a treat! We used the older chickens to make chicken and dumplings.

In summertime, the chickens would raise their little ones by themselves and we ate them when they got older. We fried young chickens and made biscuits and gravy.

We got honey from the wax in the bees' nests. We climbed the large trees where the nests were located and put silk stockings on our head and hands so they couldn't sting us.

Today, most people don't know how many months it takes for animals to have their babies, but we knew. I still know! Just ask me! A bird, two weeks. Chickens, three weeks. Ducks, four weeks. Cows, nine months. We knew it, because our folks taught us.

That was the way we lived. You would be surprised to know all the animals and ripe, wild fruit and berries we lived off of. It was all natural food compared with what we eat today, just as our exercise was natural work and play. Everything we did, more or less, kept us fit. We used our bodies to do our work and play our sports. We had no machinery, not like today. Today, it's called modern living; back then, it was called surviving.

We also hunted and caught all types of wild animals for food. We caught them and raised them. And when they had babies, we would sometimes eat the adult animals, raise the young and often make pets out of them. That was the way we survived because there was no other way to live. We knew what we had to do because winter was coming.

Our folks taught us what animals were good to hunt. In the mountains we hunted wild rabbits, squirrels, possums, frogs, birds, fox, snakes, buzzards and groundhogs, but it was very hard to find them. There weren't many of them partly because the animals ate other animals.

We went into the mountains and hunted for whatever we could catch. If we were hungry, we skinned them on the spot, built a fire and ate them right there. For our dessert, we ate birch limbs or anything we could find.

We hunted for possum and fox at night, and other animals we hunted during the day, like rabbits and squirrels. Most everything else was poison.

In summer we ate a lot of groundhogs. Groundhogs had their babies in the mountain in a big hole. Our dogs would dig them out, then we watched the dogs fight them. If there were baby groundhogs, we brought them home, raised them for pets and ate the mother. Mom knew how to cook them — she baked them in the oven!

Rabbits were very scarce. To catch them in the mountains above the coal camp, we would find a limb that we could sharpen to a point, stick it up in a hole, twist it and bring out the rabbit. Then we built a fire, skinned it and cooked it over the flames. It was fun, and it kept us from going hungry sometimes!

There weren't many fish in our river, but when we had thunderstorms, we could catch more fish. Most of the time we only caught suckers. They had a lot of bones but we ate them anyway, fried up in a frying pan in the stove with wood and coal. We also ate all the bullfrog legs and crawdad tails we could find.

There were no deer, bears or other big animals in our part of the country. There were a lot of snakes in the mountains and also in camp. Some were very poisonous.

The only time my mother went anywhere on Saturdays was to the coal camp store, but she didn't get to go too often. The store was closed on Sunday. If my mom forgot something and we needed it right then, we borrowed from the neighbors. They borrowed from us, too.

When I was young, we knew what time Mother had breakfast and supper. If we didn't get home in time to eat, we missed a meal. We either did without or helped ourselves to something out of someone's garden. We didn't destroy anything. The only time we did anything to anyone was when they treated us mean. I have to admit that we turned over a few outhouses and rocked people's houses at night.

We didn't have any bakeries — everybody did their own baking and cooking. People did all their baking at home on a wood stove. Some nights my mother made us a pot of homemade candy on the stove in an old, black skillet.

On Sunday, it was a treat to have a homemade cake. Usually there were only two kinds of cake people would bake — chocolate and white cake. But thank God, we had that.

I remember the only time I ever got a piece of cheesecake was when this Polish lady made it once a year. She always gave me a piece.
Once I stole a five-cent cake from the store. A man saw me and told my dad, so he whipped me with a big birch tree limb all the way home. I never stole from the store again.

Bananas were brought into the holler once a year, so that's when Mom would make banana pudding. We only saw watermelon once a year, too. There were never any leftovers! Sometimes oranges were shipped up the holler.

The fruit came in from a peddler who had a truck full of the kinds of fruit that we never saw unless they brought it up to the holler. When all the kids jumped on his truck to get some fruit, he got mad and gave us a good cussing. We got off the truck and let him go up the holler. While he was in the holler we went and got a crosscut saw, sawed a tree down across the road and hid in the bushes. When he came out of the holler, he couldn't get past the tree, so he yelled, "Boys, if you get the tree off the road I will give you all the fruit you want." We got our fruit, then we cleared the tree out of the road. From then on, every year when he came up the holler we got all the fruit we wanted and he got a clear road. That is how we survived.

When I was in grade school I didn't have much for lunch. We didn't have a cafeteria in the school, so I always ate by myself or didn't eat at all. We survived by eating beans and potatoes. Thank God for them, or some of us may not have had anything to eat.

We used to eat birch tree limbs. It's true! If you knew which tree was sweeter than other birch trees, you would take the small limbs and chew the bark off of them. When I tell people this they look at me like I'm crazy! We also ate such things as wild greens that grow in springtime.

The only time we got any nuts was at Christmas. We never saw English walnuts except in a little bag at Christmas time. You wouldn't believe how we appreciated the little brown bag we were given in school. We were thankful for all the little things.

We also didn't have store-bought drinks, only Kool-Aid. We even made popsicles out of snow and Kool-Aid.

Though we didn't have much, I thank God we had canned food and our pigs, chicken and cows, a sack of flour, a bag of beans, and potatoes. Anything else up in the holler we were very lucky to get, and that's the truth. That was our way of life. We thought that was the way everyone lived.

Chapter 4

Coal Camp Kids

Childhood Games

Besides hunting and fishing, we played a lot of games. Kids in the holler loved to play, and we were always glad when Saturday and Sunday came because there was no school.

We didn't have a lot of toys, so most of our activities had to do with being outdoors. As a bunch of hillbillies, we made up our own fun and games and things we played with. We did a lot outside because we didn't have gyms or any of the things kids have today. There was nothing in the holler, so we made the most of what little we had. We always appreciated everything, no matter how small it was.

We made wooden play guns by hand. I was so proud of my gun until I was riding someone's bicycle and had a wreck and broke it. Boy, was I disappointed. We glued it back together but it never worked well again.

I remember they started Cub Scouts in the holler. That was something! But most of the things we kids were involved in weren't organized.

Boys in the holler were active and very competitive in sports, even before we started going to high school. Whatever game we played, we made it a competition.

We used our bodies for everything we did, and it all pertained to good old Mother Nature. If we wanted to go somewhere we walked and ran. We had fun and it kept us in shape. I think we were in great shape compared to the kids today because we were so active.

Life was pretty much the same year-round, and all our fun depended on the weather. Spring, summer, fall or winter, we just changed our activities to fit the season.

Spring was when everything started blooming and most of the animals came out of hibernation. Possums and groundhogs hibernated until spring, and birds would go south, all except the snowbirds that loved the snow.

When springtime came, we had to change our way of living. It rained and got warm and then hot, which was very good because then you could shed most of your clothes, including your shoes.

In spring and summer, we would go into the mountains and hunt for animals to eat. We caught hawks and buzzards that made their nests in the trees in the woods, made large swings out of the winding wild grapevines, and then we would swing out over the mountains.

Way back on top of the mountains there were big oak and pine trees to climb. Some of the trees were more than 150 feet high. If you fell out of one, you were a goner. But we never thought about that.

In the summer, we did a lot of swimming and fishing in the Guyandotte River. We killed rattlesnakes, copperheads, water snakes and all poisonous snakes if we caught them around the house or in the river because we needed the river to swim in.

If we wanted to go fishing, we cut a limb out of the tree and found some string to wrap around the end and then wrapped the string around three hooks. That's what we used to snag the fish when they were still. We also set out trout lines to hook fish and picked bullfrogs from the riverbank. We ate everything we caught.

When we had a huge thunderstorm, we didn't get near the water because it would make the river get real deep. If you fell in, you were lost forever. We were taught what could happen if we fell in — it's goodbye!

When the river was down during the summer, that was our swimming hole. We dived straight out of the trees or off the bank; there were no such things as diving boards in the holler. And we gave our dogs baths in the river so they didn't stink. Did we have fun! Our swimming trunks were just cut-off pants, and if no one was around, we went in naked — but not in front of girls!

That's how we used the river: to swim, to fish, and to take baths in until it got cold.

One time, when we were still in grade school, Adolph Pedri and I were fighting with three guys, including Jimmy and Bruno Pedri (no relation to Adolph). We really wanted to get them. We had a large grapevine swing in the mountains by the river that we used to swing over the river. We knew they were coming to use it, so we climbed up and cut the vine rope so when the swing went out over the river, it would break and they would fall in.

We hid in the bushes, and while we were waiting for the boys to arrive, we weren't paying attention to the swing. We didn't notice that Dorothy Tabor and her friend started swinging. Before we could stop them, Dorothy swung out over the river and the swing broke. She went into the river and broke her leg. I felt very bad for her, but we were so scared we never told anyone. We hid under the house all day. I couldn't tell anyone or my father would have tore me up. The ambulance came. Thank God, her leg healed, and she could still walk.

Boys and girls played poker together and we sure had a lot of laughs. We played hide-and-seek, chased each other while throwing rocks (which was dangerous), and played sports like tag, baseball, basketball and football (without any pads) under the streetlight at night.

I never had a new baseball at home. We made our balls out of black miners' tape wrapped around newspaper or some other paper we could find. Our bats were made out of heavy tree limbs we cut down. Even with this primitive equipment, you wouldn't believe how hard we would practice.

We would find a place where it was flat and tear down bushes to practice our baseball swings. I guess it just came natural to us. We didn't have nice, store-bought balls to play with. In fact, I never saw a new baseball until I went to high school. It was such a treat to throw a real baseball compared to throwing rocks, which is all we had in the holler. I thought that brand-new baseball was the best!

I think maybe throwing all those rocks helped us to be able to throw a baseball fast and hard. I was a pitcher on the varsity baseball team in Mullens the four years I was in high school, and also played other positions on the team. I played two years of varsity football and basketball. I was very proud because it was such an honor to make the varsity teams. But I really played just because I loved to play.

For our basketballs, we would take a hog's bladder at hog killing time and put it in the warm attic so it would dry out. That was our basketball! We did this until we went to high school. When we saw the gym and the real basketballs, we could hardly believe our eyes!

When we played football in the holler, we just played in a dirt yard. We didn't have any equipment or even grass, just a piece of hard ground. We were really rough. That's how I got my leg broke. It happened on a

Sunday, and I had to lie on the bed all night until the next day before we went to the hospital in Beckley. In the hospital, I had to lie on my back for thirty days in traction, with a weight at the bottom of the bed to keep my leg straight. Today, they would fix it with surgery the same day.

It was the same way when I broke my arm coming off a mountain. The mountain was very steep. When I came down on my sled, I was going too fast and the bridge was so narrow that I missed it and went into the river. I had to wait until the next day to get medical attention. That wouldn't happen today.

These injuries didn't stop me from playing sports — I loved sports!

I'll bet I have climbed more trees, thrown more rocks, and made more gravel shooters (slingshots) than any kid in California.

When it snowed, you couldn't get out of the holler until it melted. People got together and played games and cards. Folks visited in one another's houses. There were no such things as cocktail parties. Most of the time, miners did their partying at the pool hall and beer joint.

Snow became our recreation. We went sledding very fast down the big mountains, slid on the river and on ice, built snowmen, had plenty of snowball battles, ate icicles, made homemade ice cream and popsicles out of Kool-Aid, and the little kids made things in the snow.

When we weren't riding our sleds, we built a big fire to keep us warm. We never really stayed in the house even if we weren't riding our sleds. No matter how cold it was, we were always outside playing or doing something.

You'd be amazed at all the things we could do in the snow. Today, there are so many distractions that keep kids from being physically active. They are on their phones and computers all the time. By not using their bodies, they will be sorry when they get old.

We should set aside all of that automation and get more exercise. I am a big believer in that. When you get older and are way overweight, you will be sorry. Ask your doctor! Take your kids out to play sports and find something that you like to do to increase your level of activity. You will live longer and feel better.

We played outdoors and stayed active because we didn't have anything else to do. When we got something as simple as a new ball, we appreciated it.

I know people today who have everything, but they still aren't happy because they have nothing to do. The worst words I hear from parents is, "I never had anything, but I want my kids to have everything I didn't have."

Parents' worst mistake is that they don't make kids work for what they want. Remember to always praise them when they do work for something. Discipline is also important, and children should learn to show respect.

Pets and Sporting Animals

There weren't a lot of animals in our area, just a few rabbits and a lot of foxes. We did eat them, so maybe that was why there weren't many of them.

We knew some people who had fox dogs to chase the foxes. I guess to the dogs' owner it was something like going to the races. The dogs were bred to hunt, and they chased the foxes through the mountains.

There was one man who worked in the coal camp and lived in the mountains who loved to hear his dogs run after the foxes. They would run all weekend long, day and night, starting at quitting time on Friday. The man built a fire and sat around while the dogs were on the hunt. His biggest itch was to see how long the dogs would chase the fox.

We went up with him sometimes, sat around the fire and listened to the dogs run after the foxes. Sometimes those dogs would run them right over our fire, but we didn't kill the foxes and we didn't eat them. They were left for the dogs to run.

If I had only known then, we would have been better off to kill the foxes because they were the ones that ate our rabbits. But we never realized it.

We knew how the man felt because we had some great fighting roosters that would fight until they died. That's what they were bred to do.

The way you learn about rooster fighting is just like dog fighting. We trained the roosters, and they fought until they killed one another. They might lie down for a minute, so tired they would lie by one another until they were rested, but then they got back up and fought until they died.

The roosters were bred so well they could be almost dead, with their heads swollen up, and they would still get back up and fight. I knew I had a great rooster to breed to the hens when that happened. If they didn't fight that way, we fried them for dinner, and that's the truth.

I learned to match a rooster with a good fighting hen. To find a good rooster, we traded good breeding roosters in Helen, Beckley and Mullens. Because we didn't have money to buy fighting chickens, we traded chickens we stole from the neighbors at night, right out of their chicken house. At the time, we didn't think it was bad. It was just the way we lived.

We caught the freight train with our sack full of chickens. We'd hop it by running and catching the ladder, and then ride it out of the holler. The hard part was getting off the train. You couldn't jump off when it was going at high speed or you could get killed.

We fought the roosters for money at locations no one knew about. The most dangerous part, and what I hated most about rooster fighting, was that some of the men would start drinking. They often carried guns or a knife and sometimes wanted to fight. Luckily, some of the other men beat the desire out of them. That stopped them.

Most people carried guns and knives back then. I don't believe it was because they were all mean, that was just the normal thing everybody did.

My uncle had a pet cat. One time I took that cat into the mountains and put lighter fluid on it, setting it on fire. It looked like a ball of fire going through the mountain. My uncle used to say, "If I find out who set my cat on fire I'll shoot him with a shotgun!"

I had a chicken and I put duck eggs under her to hatch instead of chicken eggs. When those ducks hatched from the eggs, they took to the river to swim and that mother hen went crazy, running up and down the river, trying to get them out of the water.

When a mother duck had her babies, she always took them to the river so animals couldn't eat them.

The trash dump was about a mile down the holler toward a hard, paved road. It was there that people left dogs and cats they didn't want. When we wanted a dog or cat, we got it at the dump. Not only pets, we got other things from the dump that people threw away, and we were glad to get them.

We played with all of our animals when they were babies, just like people play with toys today. We especially liked our dogs and cats. When the cats got big enough, they would catch mice or rats.

There weren't a lot of pets in the coal camp because they cost money to feed. If we didn't want our dogs or cats because we couldn't afford them anymore, we took them down to the creek and drowned them. But most of the time we kept them.

Hunting dogs were more valuable than other dogs. You either made your dogs useful or you got rid of them.

I had a big dog named Jigs who hunted cows with me and pulled me on a sled. A man in town made me a harness that I put on Jigs and hitched up to the sled, and away I would go.

We had all types of hunting dogs. It was great to have a good one that would run animals into a hole or up a tree and keep them there until we got to them. Most animals we caught were taken home to eat.

If you had a mean dog, you kept it chained up. Most of the time, if a dog was mean, someone would kill it with poison or a shotgun. Rat poison killed a lot of dogs.

Our other animals were baby groundhogs. We raised them and made pets out of them. They sucked on medicine bottles until they got big. We also brought home rabbits and snakes for pets.

We had to climb trees to get the big black snakes called blue racers. Some of them were six feet long. They would catch their prey, wrap their body around it and suffocate it. We used to catch them and play with them. We even let them wrap themselves around our arms. When they got too tight, we squeezed their heads to cut off their air, and they would relax and let go.

When we caught baby snakes and lizards, we put them into fruit jars with holes in the lid so they could get air. We made pets out of them and played with them. When they got big, we let them loose on the high top of the mountains.

Our dogs and cats knew to stay outside and not come in the house unless we brought them in. But today, people talk about their animals like they are children. They have animal hospitals, grooming and all these modern ways of babying their pets. Back then, all we did with our animals was use them for hunting or to play with. We never treated them like family!

Holidays and Seasons

We had four seasons in West Virginia — spring, summer, fall and winter — and you can bet your boots those seasons would come. We had some terrible snowstorms in the winter and thunderstorms in the summer. At times they could be very dangerous.

We learned to respect those four seasons or it could be bad for us. We knew what we had to do to survive. It was hard work, but it was the way we had to live.

There were certain things we could do only during spring and summer, but when it turned autumn and winter, there was a big change. There was only so much we could do outside in the snow and ice. We wore "long-handle" underwear (long johns), which sure came in handy.

In the summertime, folks took their shoes off and saved them for cold weather. When I started going to high school, we always wore shoes but no long underwear on account of the teasing. Wearing long underwear was a sign we were poor, and everybody teased us.

In wintertime, besides riding sleds down the mountains and having snowball battles, we made snowmen, with a piece of coal for their eyes, ears and mouth, and black buttons down the middle.

The pool hall and poker games were very popular, because when you had a big snow storm nobody could drive anywhere (if you had a car), and sometimes it was so cold that cars wouldn't even start. When the weather got that bad, you had to walk wherever you were going.

We spent a lot of time in the mountains in the spring, summer and fall of the year, but we couldn't go very high into the mountains during the winter because the snow was very deep. There was also plenty of snow around our house.

Sometimes on Halloween night things became violent. People turned over outhouses and threw rocks at the homes of people they didn't like. They also had rock-throwing battles, and that could be dangerous.

We appreciated holidays back then. Since there was no such thing as going out to dinner in the coal camp, we would have a different, special kind of dinner at home.

One of the best treats I ever got was when the school gave out a bag of nuts, an apple, an orange, and hard candy for Christmas. We never saw English walnuts or hard candy except at Christmas, if we were lucky. That's what made it such a treat. You had to use a hammer to crack open the walnuts.

We were lucky on Christmas because we usually each got one gift, but we never got it until Christmas morning. Mother always waited to put out the presents until we all went to bed. We were always excited! Even if we only got a red rubber ball, we appreciated whatever we got.

The Christmas we got the rubber ball, we played with it all day because all we had were ones made out of black tape from the coal mines.

The very best part of Christmas was my dad not getting drunk and raising hell all day. And if there was a big snow on the ground, we went out and rode our sleds or made a snowman.

Everything was done according to the season and weather. We took what Mother Nature gave us — that was our treat, and it was all we knew.

Chapter 5

Around the Holler

The New Cabin

At one point during my childhood, Dad moved us into a little cabin two miles farther up in the holler, back into the mountains. I couldn't believe it. It was so far up that we had no lights except kerosene lanterns. We had no electricity, but we did have a wood stove and, of course, outside toilets. The cabin was very small, with dark blue paper on the walls.

You just don't realize what it was like in those mountains. We were all by ourselves with no close neighbors to play with or even see. There were no other kids around, so we pretty much had to entertain ourselves until we went to school.

We could hear the freight train blowing its horn as it passed in the distance, its sound carrying over the mountains. It was an awful lonesome sound, and it sure was lonely with no one around but our own family.

In fact, we were living in this cabin when Dad had the accident on the slate car that broke his leg.

It didn't matter how far out we were, we still had to walk everywhere. Even when it snowed, we had to walk out of those hills to get to school.

We only lived there about two years, then Dad finally got smart and we moved right back into the same house we had moved out of. You can imagine how happy we kids were that we finally had friends to play with again. We were tickled to death to have electricity, and Mom was glad to be back in the camp where she could shop more easily.

Church in the Holler

We had morning devotions in school, which was good because our folks never took us to church when we were growing up.

We never went to church, and no one ever mentioned anything about going to church. Mom had so many kids to take care of that she didn't have time to go to church.

At home we had no teaching in regards to religion. That's not a good thing to say about my family, but it is true.

There was so much hell-raising going on at home, it's another reason I was glad to get out of there and start my own life.

Even though we never attended, there was the Wyco Church in the holler and a Catholic church seven miles away in Mullens.

Wyco Church was built in 1917. It's had other names over the years: Wyco Community Church, Wyco Independent Church, Wyco Freewill Baptist Church and Wyco Independent Baptist Church.

That church was there when I was born and it is still standing today, overlooking Allen Creek. Now they are making it into a monument to the holler. It is being restored and turned into a coal camp museum. It is now owned by an organization called the Rural Appalachian Improvement League, located in Mullens, and was put on the National Register of Historic Places in 2010.

The church has stood there for almost 100 years. I think it should stand forever to show that God was there for the miners and all the people and families who lived in the holler. I believe God left it there because He knows there is still faith in the holler.

Looking back, I think our parents never talked about church or took us to church because they were just trying to survive. I really believe that deep down, they loved the Lord Jesus with all their hearts.

I'm afraid that people today have forgotten about the most important thing in our life, and that's the Lord Jesus Christ.

Hometown Sons

At least one Wyco boy became famous. Bernie Casey became a football player, track and field athlete and an actor on television and in movies.

World War II veteran Basil Kester wasn't world famous, but he was a big deal in the holler. In 1942, Kester was part of the Philippines Bataan Death March. I remember he was nothing but skin and bones when he came back home to the States. They put weight back on him so fast that his skin and face looked like baby fat.

We never really knew what he went through until years later. They should have given him a big heroes' welcome with a marching band. But back then, living so far up in the holler, we were ignorant about such things. We did let him know that we were proud of him and of all our soldiers who served in World War II. That is why I write about them now, because we should be thankful for all they sacrificed and tell them how proud we are of them.

After he had been home for a while he married a gal in the holler and went to work in the mines.

When I was about sixteen years old, my two older brothers joined the military to serve in World War II. People were proud to serve their country. We never saw them when they were gone to war, but mom always wrote to them.

There were some great basketball players who came from West Virginia, including pro player Rod Thorn. I think because it is so cold, rainy and snowy outside and you have to stay inside that it gives people a lot of time to practice.

Basketball was about the only sport we had in the winter. It was too cold and stormy to do any kind of swimming sports or track and field, although we did some of those things when it got warmer in the summer.

My future high school coach, Lewis D'Antoni, was from Mullens. He graduated from Mullens High School and came back from college to Mullens during the summer to play baseball against teams from other towns in the area. He returned to Mullens as a coach in 1942, leaving a few months later to serve in the Navy in World War II. In 1946, he was back at Mullens High School, teaching biology and coaching our football, basketball and baseball teams. He even became the school principal twelve years later.

Coach D'Antoni wrote a book in 2011 about his life, "The Coach's Coach," and inscribed a copy to me:

"To Darrell, the young man that came out of Wyco hollow, that left for Calif. with three dollars and made it big. Enjoyed being your coach. Best wishes, Lewis D'Antoni."

He was a great coach!

Part 2

MULLENS HIGH SCHOOL

Chapter 6

High School Years

When I graduated from eighth grade, there was no one except me and my mother walking down the railroad tracks in the pitch dark to get home. It was so dark you couldn't see your hand in front of your face.

She said, "Darrell, you graduate high school for me."

I never forgot that. She was my hero.

Mullens is located at the junction of state highways 10, 16 and 54, where the Slab Fork Creek joins the Guyandotte River. In fact, on the cover of this book is a picture of the Slab Fork at Mullens.

A lot of people from the holler went to Mullens on the weekends. It was the biggest town near us. My father never had a car, so we had to hitchhike or walk out of the holler seven miles down a dirt road to reach Mullens.

But when we got out of eighth grade, it was something great to go to Mullens High School and ride the bus every day. It was the first time I ever rode on a bus. It was such a change from elementary school.

High school was a big surprise for me. I couldn't believe how big it was. The first gym I ever saw was at Mullens High School. And besides the gym, there was a beautiful grass football field and baseball field.

Boy, did we have fun! At first, all I thought about was sports, but then I met a lot of girls and started dating. It was very hard to meet someone to date in the holler because people didn't get out much. It was like one big family there.

Being in high school was like a dream — everything was better than grade school. When we started playing sports and chasing those girls, we never thought about the holler anymore. It was a different world, with real sports and a real town instead of a little coal camp.

You wouldn't believe the clothes (or lack of) that I wore. I didn't have fancy things like some of those kids had. I had to wear hand-me-downs or I borrowed my brother Robert's clothes when he let me.

Thank God, we had Robert. He was the one who helped support us and helped me through school. He also left me money to buy my meal ticket at the cafeteria. There were so many kids in the family — just imagine getting all those kids ready for school. We learned to help one another.

There's an old saying, "Where there's a will, there's a way." And back then, even if you got one little thing, you appreciated it very much.

In high school, I was embarrassed about my hands smelling like the cows after I'd been milking. I got that cow stain on my hands and when I was playing sports and got sweaty, boy, would it stink! I smelled like a cow!

When I told my dad, he said, "I don't need you to milk those cows," and he told my brother Jake to milk them. But in about three months the cows started going dry because Jake wasn't milking them right, so Dad sold them and I never had to milk cows again. I sure was glad of that.

Lunchtime was a little tricky. A high school meal ticket cost a dollar for the week, but our scrip coins were only worth 75 cents. A lot of times, Mama wouldn't have any lunch for us, and we didn't want to eat some hard cornbread.

So when I didn't have a lunch and no money to buy anything, my buddy Pete Bishop and I would steal a lunch out of someone's locker. We also got sandwiches out of our girlfriends' lockers. We always knew who had a great lunch.

And just for fun we used to catch black snakes put them in the girls' lockers — talk about screaming!

Sports

All the boys couldn't wait to go to high school and try out to play sports. Even though I never saw a new baseball until I was in high school, we were used to throwing rocks in the holler. We had some good ballplayers come out of the holler.

I never saw a basketball gym until I was in the ninth grade. I couldn't believe how nice it was, and how easy it was to dribble the basketball on the polished wood floor compared to the hard dirt, rocks and freezing cold we were used to. And the football field was beautiful with its green grass.

For what we had to work with in the holler, we did pretty well in sports. We didn't have any grass to practice on, it was just the hard, cold ground, and most of the time there was rain or frost covering it. But that didn't stop us from playing tackle football or basketball. We were in good physical shape from running, throwing rocks and climbing trees — anything you could do outdoors.

Here were all of us hillbillies coming out of that holler and getting to play organized sports. It was an honor to make it on the football, basketball or baseball squad. It was really something to make the team, and it didn't hurt that all the girls liked ballplayers. I played two years of varsity football and four years of varsity baseball. It was such a great honor to make the varsity teams, earn a letter and wear that sweater.

We had some great coaches, like Coach Lewis D'Antoni, who coached our football, baseball and basketball teams. He was such a nice person and he always spoke very kindly. So did our other basketball coach, Coach Wyatt.

I really believe if it hadn't been for getting to play on the high school sports teams, I probably would have ended up being a pool hustler. The only reason I stayed in school was sports and to graduate for my mother. And there was one more reason, my girlfriend Geneva Cassanelli. She gave me a lot of encouragement to graduate.

Whatever the sport — football or baseball — a lot of times after practice we would have to walk over that big, high mountain to get home. I played all the sports, so after I got done practicing after school I either hitchhiked seven miles home or walked three miles over the mountain.

During my childhood a lot of people in Wyco thought they were too good to play with the Wilcox kids. But when we got in high school, we showed them how to do great in sports. The only thing I wish is that I could have brought some of my friends home with me to spend the night, but we didn't have room and I was scared of my old man coming in and raising hell. But it was so nice and peaceful when I got to spend the night with my friends.

I remember one time after the homecoming football game we all went out to a little place and had a party, and someone brought a bottle of wine. When the coach found out about it, he got the whole football team together and made us run up and down those football bleachers all week. We never did find out who brought the bottle of wine, but one thing I can say is we never did that again. I'd already had enough of my dad drinking at home.

I'm sad to say that my folks never saw me and my high school team play because they didn't have a car to get to the games. Even though they never saw me play, many people on the streets of Mullens would compliment me on how I played.

Having Fun

All our special events took place in the gym, including dances.

During my senior year I needed some help taking my English test, so I told the principal's daughter that if she helped me I would take her to the senior prom. She let me see the answers on her paper. I didn't get caught, but I never did take her to the prom. I should have, but I didn't.

Instead, I took Geneva to the prom. I never thought about dancing when I was growing up, and when I was at the prom with Geneva, I never thought about asking her to dance. But all of a sudden she said, "Darrell, do you know what I don't like is someone who doesn't like to dance." After thinking about it a minute, I said, "Do you want to dance?" and we started dancing right then! I loved it, and I couldn't wait to go to the dances after that.

Back then the boys all thought if you danced you were a sissy. But I like to dance and most women love to dance, too. It was things like sports and dancing that kept me in school. I've liked dancing ever since, and I turned out to be a good dancer. I love it to this day.

All the girls in high school came to the ballgames. We also took them out to the movies, walking to their house to get them and then walking them home. We walked everywhere because no one had a car.

Anytime I wasn't busy playing sports, I went pool hustling. I was good at shooting pool and made some money at it going to different towns in the area.

One Saturday, I had a date with Betty Robinette, but I didn't have any money. There were two miners who were shooting pool, and I got in the game. I had some luck that day and cut a five-ball backwards. Even to this day I don't know how I made that ball. But I won, and it is a good thing I did, because I didn't have any money to pay them. If I had lost, they would have whipped me. I grabbed that money and we took off to the movies.

Even though I was a good pool player, what I really wanted to do was be a barber. When you become a senior, they ask you what you want to do. When I told them, some of them laughed at me. But I showed them!

Geneva was a nice girl and we had a good time together. She showed me how to save my money, and I became very efficient with it. To this day I still am very conservative with my money. She taught me that. She was a great lady.

Her dad owned some theaters, and we got in free. Geneva's sister Mary let us use her car sometimes. Isn't that something! Hardly anybody had a car back then, but today everybody has a car, even the high school kids.

Maybe I didn't have a car, but I rode a motorbike. Only one problem — it wasn't mine. The bike belonged to Glenn Castleman, whose dad was a big superintendent of the mines. They were rich! My friend Pete Bishop said, "I can run a motorbike. Let's take it!"

We climbed on it and took off way in the mountains. Coming down one big mountain called Pierpont, we got a flat. We were flying down the mountain on a flat tire!

Pete said, "Darrell, you gotta get off!"

I was thrown head over heels and was lucky I didn't get killed. He stopped the bike, and we threw it in the bushes.

The Family Graduate

The Wyco miners often told me, "Darrell, I'm glad you're going to high school." Even so, some of them didn't think I would go to barber school, though that's all I thought about.

I also had Geneva behind me all the way. She always stood by me and encouraged me. Even when I went to barber school, guess who took me? It was Geneva and Mary. When you had people like them, it was super! They really encouraged me and I have never forgotten that. Thank God, I had them to encourage me and help me.

I was the first and only one in my family who graduated from high school. I almost quit a few times, but my mother asked me if I would graduate for her, and I did. I was her only child who graduated. She also said one time, "You know, Darrell, I never worry about you."

Even though no one ever came to watch me play sports — not my mother, dad or anybody — my mother did come to see me graduate from high school.

After graduating, I got a scholarship to pitch baseball at Concord College, but I only went three days. You see, I had to hitchhike to school and it was very difficult. Besides, it just wasn't what I wanted to do. So I quit, hitchhiked home and figured out how to become a barber.

I knew I was going to have to go to work loading coal in the coal mines if I wanted to make any money, because there was no other work in the holler. I didn't want to, but I had no other way of earning money for school.

I came home, went to work and saved my money so I could get out of the holler.

The mines were dangerous, and I was scared. But as soon as I had enough money to pay my tuition to barber school, I got out of there.

Part 3

THE MINE

Chapter 7

Working in the Coal Mine

The mine and coal camp at Wyco were built in 1914, by the Wyoming Coal Company.

I went to work in the mine about 1950, and saved up for barber school. I was only eighteen years old when I started working, and it was the only way I could make some money.

I planned to be in the mine a year, but I worked thirteen months. As soon as I saved enough, I got out of there! I quit the mines and went to school as soon as I could. I was thankful I didn't get hurt bad or killed, because a lot of men did.

Just think about the miners in the 2010 Copaipo Mine cave-in in Chile, and how they lived through their experience being trapped underground for 69 days. Even with today's mine disasters, I think things are better for the most part than they were about sixty years ago when I was in the mines.

Today, they have all types of machinery in the mines to work with. They go straight down into the mines on conveyors, and machines load the coal. They also have a lot better protection.

Back when I was in the mine, we rode on flat cars called "man trips" that were pulled by a motor about two miles deep inside the mine to our stations.

Each car could carry six people. Because the roof of the mine was so low, we had to lie down flat, which wasn't very comfortable. We didn't dare try to sit up because we could get our heads knocked off.

Since the mine was only about four feet to five feet tall, most of the workday was spent on our knees or stooped over and bent down below our hips. It was hard work!

At the end of the workday we walked on our knees back to our station, where a flat car picked us up to go outside. You can't imagine how hard we worked in there.

Clothes and Equipment

We lived about three-quarters of mile from the miners' bathhouse, where we kept the clothes we worked in. It was a large building that had about sixteen showers.

The bathhouse had high ceilings — that way we could hang our clothes individually. It was where we dressed for work. Then after work, we took a shower, changed into our regular clothes and hung up our dirty work clothes to wear the next day.

It was so cold inside the mine that we wore long-handle underwear all year-round. The inside temperature never changed, it just stayed the same all year long.

Every day, you put on your work clothes: the long-handle underwear, overhauls (overalls), boots and the hard shell hat with the lamp. We also had kneepads because we worked on our knees all the time.

We wore hard-toed boots to protect our feet from rocks that fell down from the top or walls of the mineshaft. A big sandstone rock could easily break your foot or leg. And there was no way we could work without our gloves.

Outside the bathhouse was a lamp house where we charged the battery for the light that was on our hard hat. We wore the battery on our back, down by our hip. The little light wasn't much, but we never thought about it because that was the way it had always been, and it was all we knew. Those lights were the only way we could see to work in the mines. In fact, there were no other lights anywhere in the mine, so you can imagine it was pretty dark as we worked.

The Work Process

Working in the mine was the same thing every day. We'd get there early in the morning and walk down to the mine or to the shower house where we changed into our work clothes.

We rode the man trip or coal car down a track deep into the mine, where it stopped at the main head where we worked. We got out and walked stooped-over to our stations, or "holes," as we called them.

They used large fans to pump fresh air to us way back in the mine. You could see the fans at the hole we went back in. If those fans ever stopped, we would have been goners.

We used dynamite to shoot our coal, and placed timbers to keep the roof and sides of the work area from falling in on us.

In our small work holes, walking on our knees with a pair of kneepads, we loaded our coal with the help of a No. 4 shovel, which has a wide, square blade. We worked our areas alone, breaking up the coal and loading it by ourselves. Each worker was assigned his own area to work.

Besides loading the coal and setting the wood timbers, we had to separate the rock out of the coal before loading it into the car.

The only other people we saw all day were the motor and brakeman, who came to pull our full coal car out and bring in another empty car to fill. I could load five or six cars a day by myself.

With no one to talk to, it was pretty lonely back in the hole. Once you got into your area there were no coffee breaks or lunch hour — all you did was work.

The coal mine was a very busy place. Most of the miners worked inside, but I think working on the outside was a lot easier.

At the end of our shift we had to knee-walk back to the station, where we rode the motor and flat cars out of the mine.

Tipple

In the holler there was one small creek, which grew larger when it rained really hard. There was also a river that came out of the mines and flowed with black water. It was where the miners dumped their water from the "tipple."

When the coal came out on a flat car, it was taken to the tipple. There, coal was separated from the bone and rock. The coal was then sorted according to size by being sent through different-sized screens.

The sorted coal went into large railroad cars, and the train came up the holler and hauled it out. The only reason we had railroad tracks in the holler was so they could load the coal cars for delivery to different parts of the country.

Pretty much all the work in the tipple was high up in the air. We had to be careful because it was easy to fall out of the tipple.

The tipple got its name from the way workers pushed the coal carts to the area where they were unloaded and tipped them to dump out the coal.

Coal from the mines was taken to Mullens and shipped out by train in big coal cars. Even though they used trains to ship the coal, there were never any passenger trains that came to Mullens. The closest passenger trains were in Princeton, West Virginia, the town that pro basketball player Rod Thorn was from.

A lot of times the coal train was how we got a ride out of the holler. Even though it was against the law, the engineers never said anything because they knew we needed a ride.

Working Together

You need to remember that in those days there was still racial segregation. The black miners lived in one coal camp, and we lived in another. We also had separate bathhouse shower rooms.

Blacks and whites didn't have big conflicts or hard feelings as we worked in the mines together. They were real good in sports and we often played together.

One time there was a bad incident among three black miners. One man used to ride back and forth to work in the back of a pickup owned by two brothers. The two brothers thought it was funny to take the other man's lunch pail, eat his food and then laugh at him.

The man got tired of it, so one day, he waited until the two brothers got in the shower, then he went in and shot them both.

That was the worst thing I can remember.

In the coal mine, I have to say that the black miners who worked with me watched over me better than the white miners. They protected me.

I was there three months when I got a dig place near Moore, a short black man. He would shine his light in my hole two or three times a day to make sure I was alive. He was always watching me, checking on me, and I was grateful he did.

Another good guy, the brakeman Tom Ross, was a black man.

In the black community, they had their own pool hall and beer joint. If there was ever a fight, I never heard a thing about it.

I found most of them to be really great people and hard workers.

Dangers

Terrible things happened in the mines. You can't go two or three miles into a mountain and not find danger. It is really scary because so many things can happen to you in there.

Mines have explosive gas in them. Some of the miners smoked in the mine, even though they knew it was against the rules and could have blown us all up.

The most dangerous thing that ever happened to me in the mine happened on a Friday. On Fridays, the miners tried to get their six cars loaded and get out of there as fast as possible. I was getting ready to shoot my coal, and in my hurry I forgot to keep my wires together. They were lying open on the tracks where the motor was, and they were hot. If I hadn't touched my hand to one of the hot wires and realized it, they could have blown up and covered me with coal. I was very lucky.

Another time, one of my friends, Ransom Taylor, was working as a brakeman on the motor and got killed when the flat car turned over on him. He was smart and wanted to go to school to be a lawyer, but he never got the chance.

Another danger was coal dust. Miners didn't live long lives because of the rock and coal dust that they breathed five days a week. After a few years, the lungs get so hard that it's very difficult to breathe. This was common in coal miners. Black lung disease cut short many miners' lives. We just accepted it because it was all we knew, and mining was our way of life.

The miners took it for granted that getting hurt or even killed went along with the job, but I sure learned a lot different when I finally got out of there.

People from the holler never really thought of any other work except the mine, because there just wasn't anything else to do. There weren't a lot of opportunities in the hills where we lived.

I don't want to give the impression that we were all dumb. We got a good education in the holler, and the teachers were great, even though our school only went through the eighth grade.

I am glad we have better protection for our miners in America today. I really feel sorry for the people who worked in the mines in China. They lost 2,600 miners in one year. That is uncalled for.

End of the Workday

The workday was over at about 4 p.m. After working all day on our knees, we had to carry our dinner buckets and the bag that held our dynamite to shoot the coal, and then walk bent-over half the length of the mine to ride the car out of the mine. We didn't want to be late or we would have to walk the whole two miles out.

Once we finally got out of the mine, our day still wasn't over. We had to put our batteries on the charger for the next day and then go to the bathhouse and take a shower because we were black head to toe from coal dust. In fact, everything around the mine was covered with coal dust.

After a shower, we changed our clothes and got everything ready for the next day's work. We didn't change into clean work clothes every day, we just put on the same clothes and went back to work in them. We kept our clean clothes in the bathhouse and never wore dirty work clothes home.

Once I showered and changed into my street clothes, I still had to walk almost a mile home. Working in the mines is very tiring. When I got home at night, all I thought about was eating dinner, going to sleep and resting for the next day of work. Early the next morning it was time to get up and start all over again.

That was the routine every day of the workweek, until Friday. On the weekend from Friday night to Sunday night, the miners "let it all hang out," as they called it, which usually included drinking and playing cards or pool.

I always looked forward to Friday because it was wonderful to have the weekend to get off of my knees, rest, have a little fun and unwind from a hard week.

Weekends

The coal miners worked Monday through Friday and were off on Saturday and Sunday. On the weekends, we either stayed home and rested or went down to the beer joint and pool hall to get drunk or find a poker game. That was all there was to do in Wyco holler when you didn't have a car.

There were no bars in West Virginia back then, but they had liquor stores, beer joints and pool halls where they also played poker. There were a lot of fights in the pool hall.

Once some men were playing poker in the pool hall owned by Tuck Armontrout. Big John Bailey was playing, and he lost all his money to Dude Mullen that day. He was mad, so he went home and got his shotgun and came back to shoot Dude, but he couldn't find him. Tuck was talking to his partner on the telephone, and Big John was so mad that he shot Tuck and blew his head off. Tuck hadn't done a thing to him — Big John was mad because he lost his money in the pool hall.

Miners played poker from Friday night to Sunday night, depending on how much money they had. Sometimes we didn't stop until Monday morning. We could play all day and night on Saturday or Sunday, but Monday morning, everyone had to get ready to go to work. There was never any partying on weekdays. When you come out of the mines you went home and rested up for the next day.

Pool hustling, poker playing and gambling were a few of the ways we survived. I loved the challenge of playing sports and gambling, but in business, I always did things right and professionally.

While the only liquor you could buy in the holler was beer, you could buy hard liquor in Mullens. If you had a car, you could go to Mullens, where it was always busy Friday and Saturday nights. Miners liked to go there on weekends if they had a ride and some money.

With people coming out of the holler every weekend, Mullens was quite busy. Everyone — not just miners, but husbands and wives, too — stood on Main Street and visited with one another.

Out of the Mine and Out of the Holler

About the middle of December on the last day I was supposed to work in the mine, there was a big snow on the ground. My brothers and my dad had already left for work when my mother said to me, "Darrell, you know how Dominic Jones got killed? It was his last day at the mine for him, and a big rock fell on him and killed him!"

She was scared for me and said, "Why don't you stay home and not work in the mine on your last day?"

My mom was always the greatest. I did exactly what she wanted me to do.

And I didn't miss that job one little bit. I guess I was lucky to get to work in the mines for thirteen months so I could make enough money to go to barber school.

I was glad to get out of the holler, and my family was probably happy to see me go. When we got to a certain age, my dad and mother didn't mind when we kids left home because there were so many of us. When you had as many kids in the family as we did, they were glad to see you go. It wasn't because Mom didn't love us. I know she did.

I moved away at the age of nineteen, and we still didn't have a phone, a car, or anything like that. When I went to barber college, no one came to see me leave except my friend Joe Dillon's mom and dad. That was just the way it was.

Top: My father, Walter "Red" Wilcox.

Bottom: My mother, Carrie (Gillen) Wilcox.

Top: This is a drawing of my father,
Walter "Red" Wilcox, as a child.

Bottom: One of these men is my grandfather,
I'm not sure which one.

WEST VIRGINIA STATE DEPARTMENT OF HEALTH

County of _Wyoming_

District of _Slab Fork_

	CERTIFICATE OF BIRTH OR STILLBIRTH	**38954**
		(For State Reg. use only)

Town or City of _Wyco, W Va_ No._____ St._____
(If birth occurred in a hospital or institution, give its NAME instead of street and number)

2. Full Name of Child _Dearrel Edward Wilcox_
(Do not write in this space if child is not yet named)
(If child is not yet named, make supplemental report, of name, later.)

3. Sex of Child _male_

4. Is this child a Twin or Triplet _no_

5. If twin give number in order of birth.

6. Premature Full term _yes_

7. Are parents Married? _yes_

8. Date of birth _12-28_ 19_31_ (Month) (Day) (Year)

FATHER	MOTHER
9. Full Name _Wilcox, Walter Lee_	18. Name Before Marriage _Gillen, Carrie_
10. P. O. Address _Wyco, W Va_	19. P. O. Address _Wyco, W Va_
11. Color or Race _white_ 12. Age at last birthday _29_ (Years)	20. Color or Race _white_ 21. Age at last birthday _25_ (Years)
13. Birthplace _Va_	22. Birthplace _Va_

OCCUPATION

14. Trade, profession, or particular kind of work done, as spinner, sawyer, bookkeeper, etc. _Coal mines_

15. Industry or business in which work was done, as silk mill, sawmill, bank, etc.

16. Date (month and year) last engaged in this work _____ 19__

17. Total time (years) spent in this work

23. Trade, profession, or particular kind of work done, as housekeeper, typist, nurse, clerk, etc. _House Wife_

24. Industry or business in which work was done, as own home, lawyer's office, silk mill, etc.

25. Date (month and year) last engaged in this work _____ 19__

26. Total time (years) spent in this work

27. Did you place in each eye of the baby, a one per cent solution of Nitrate of Silver immediately after birth? _yes_

28. Please list the number of children born to this mother according to (a) (b) (c)

(a) Born alive and now living _4_
(b) Born alive and now dead _1_
(c) Stillborn _0_

IF STILLBORN

29. Period of gestation _9_ (Months)

30. Cause of Stillbirth _____

Before Labor _____
During Labor _____

CERTIFICATE OF ATTENDING PHYSICIAN OR MIDWIFE

I hereby certify that I attended the birth of this child, who was _Born alive_ at _10_ P. M,
on the date above stated. (Born alive or stillborn) (Hours A. M. or P. M.)

*When there was no attending physician or midwife, then the father, or mother, should make this return.

(Signature) _Darrell D. Wilkinson_
(Physician, Midwife, Parent)

Filed _JAN 10 1932_ 19__

H. C. Figliosino Registrar

Wyco, W Va Address

This is a copy of my original birth certificate
with my name misspelled.

Top: The bridge (lower left) where I broke my arm
while sledding.

Bottom: The Wilcox house (on the right) in Wyco.

Miners of Wyco Coal Company

Walter "Red" Wilcox is standing near center of
bottom picture with arms folded (arrow).

Top: Dr. Darrell Wilkinson and family.

Bottom: Dr. Wilkinson's family home above the
Wyco coal camp.

Top: Wyco mine superintendent's home.

Bottom: Wyco Church.

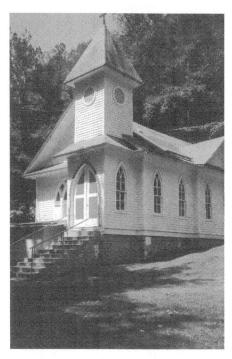

Top: Wyco black families' church.

Bottom: Wyco boarding house.

Top: Wyco Grade School (unknown children).

Bottom: My certificate for completing eight books of the West Virginia primary reading circle (1939).

Wyoming County Schools
PINEVILLE, WEST VIRGINIA
Pupils Reading Circle

This is to Certify that _____ Darrell Wilcox _____

of the _____ Wyco _____ Grade School,

having completed _____ eight _____ Books of the West Virginia Primary Reading Circle is entitled to this

CERTIFICATION OF ACHIEVEMENT

Certified by Authority of _____

_____ W. A. Bailey Jr. _____   _____ J. B. McGraw _____
COUNTY SUPERINTENDENT   PRINCIPAL

Dated _____ May 19, _____ 1939   _____ Hazel D. Toler _____
TEACHER

Top: General store in Wyco.

Bottom: Mullens High School.

Top: Mullens, West Virginia.

Bottom: Mullens, 1949.

Top: My barber college diploma.

Bottom: My Petty Officer Second Class training certificate from the U.S. Naval Training Center, San Diego, California.

Top: Graduation from Petty Officers training school, 1952.

Bottom: In Navy uniform.

Top: USS Kearsarge (CVA-33), circa 1952-55.

Bottom: Navy days with my shipmates.

In the Navy.

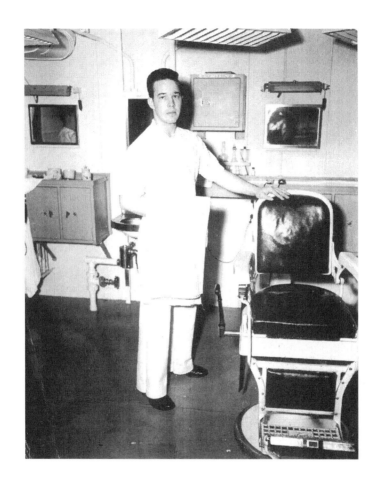

Working as a Navy barber on the USS Kearsarge.

Top: Darrell and Dorothy Wilcox.

Bottom: Dorothy and me enjoying a swim.

Top: The Wilcox family with Dorothy's parents.

Bottom: The Wilcox kids,
Darla, Darrell Jr. and Kim.

A few golf tournaments I played in.

Top: My official California barber identification picture.

Bottom: Santa Fe Golf Driving Range.
(Built and owned by me and my wife Sherma.)

Top: I am holding a 1949 picture of
Wyco coal miners.

Bottom: Darrell and Sherma Wilcox.

Part 4

LEAVING HOME

Chapter 8

Barber College

From a very young age, going to barber school was one of the most important things in my life. I wanted to prove to those people back home that I could finish school and become a barber.

I left Wyco holler in 1951, and went to school in Cincinnati, Ohio. The tuition was $569 for a ten-month course of study, and I had $1,300 saved, thanks to my girlfriend Geneva Cassanelli and her sister Mary. When I got ready to go, Geneva and Mary took me to catch the train.

I was really excited to be on my way, but I had never been so scared. I didn't tell anyone, but maybe it showed, because a man on the train said, "If you want to hold on to me, I will let you know when we get there."

A lot of people in the holler and Mullens didn't think I would go, but I fooled them.

Until I got there, I didn't realize how big a city Cincinnati was. But people were very good to me, and I quickly learned how to survive.

The first few days, I learned a lot about where to live — and where not to live. They took me to the YMCA to stay. It was only $4.50 a week for one room, which was better than living on skid row where the barber college was located.

I didn't know how dangerous skid row was until they told me it was where all the bums and winos lived. They wound up being the people we practiced giving free haircuts to, besides our fellow students at the school.

People just don't realize how much there is to learn in barber school. We not only learned to cut hair, we also learned to give shaves, massages, facials, a singe, vibrator massage and how to apply tonic.

It was a very professional school, open eight hours a day and five days a week. For the first week or so we studied our books. I didn't like that at all until my instructor told me I would soon get on a barber chair and do my studies on the side. That was great to hear!

While I was in school, I ran into a lot of veterans from World War II, and the Korean War had just started.

One of the funniest things that happened in school was when my buddy got a bum in his chair at 8 a.m. He was still working on the bum at noon, and the man was cussing at him. Finally my buddy asked the instructor, "When do you finish cutting? I don't know when I am finished!"

It may be hard to believe, but when I was going to barber school, there were times I didn't have enough money to buy breakfast or lunch. Every day I had to figure out where I could get something to eat. My poor mom sometimes sent me things in a box from home. I never told her that the food was hard by the time it arrived and I couldn't eat it. I just told her how good it was because I loved her so much.

Thank God for the three kids who had a restaurant next door. They were very good to me, taking me home with them in the evening. And when their sister came in, she always gave me a sandwich to eat.

They fed me until a friend gave me his night job at the hotel Sheridan Gibson, the largest hotel in Cincinnati. What a relief! It was a lifesaver, and I sure appreciated it. That job helped me finish barber school.

At night after school was done, I worked in the hotel cocktail lounge until 2 a.m. They started me working in the basement downstairs, but it wasn't long before they moved me up with the bartenders and I learned to make drinks. I read a book on mixing drinks whenever I had time.

Soon, I was working behind the bar and knew how to make all the drinks men and women liked best.

I met a lot of nice people — not only those who worked at the hotel, but people from all over the world who stayed there and visited the bar. As I got acquainted with them, talking to them as I mixed the drinks, I began to receive a lot of tips. I was doing so well that it wasn't long before our bosses made everyone who worked at the bar split the tips.

The most embarrassing thing that ever happened to me at the bar was the time a woman ordered a sloe gin and tonic. Sloe gin is red, but I gave her white gin. The bartender I worked with got a big kick out of that.

When I finished my shift at 2 a.m., I ran the switchboard for the YMCA in exchange for my room, which saved me $4.50 a week.

I had to walk from the hotel to the YMCA, which was about a mile. It was very late, of course, and every night this guy would jump out of the bushes by the highway. I told the hotel chef about it one night, and he gave me one of his big butcher knives to carry. When the guy jumped out of the bushes, I showed him the knife, and it scared him so bad that he ran like hell. I never saw him again.

For recreation, I played softball and baseball with the YMCA and the Baptist church. I made lot of friends in barber school, at the YMCA, and playing sports. Working at the hotel was also a lot of fun.

Some funny things happened while I was in school. Once, this old guy was in my chair getting a shave, and he was telling me all about his girlfriend. He kept raising his head up, and the instructor told him to keep his head down. I turned to the sink, and all of a sudden he rose up and the razor hit him right across the nose. Blood flew everywhere!

The instructor threw him out and put someone else in my chair, saying, "Don't worry about it. It's his own fault for lifting his head up."

Even in Cincinnati, I was a good pool player and loved to play for money. There was a man who wanted me to quit school and go pool hustling. We also became good poker players.

Sometimes, it was a real temptation to gamble or play pool professionally, because it was a very depressed situation at home and there were so many of us kids. But I believe that God had a plan for me to become a barber instead.

I finally worked my way up from number four chair to number one. I made it, with a lot of hard work and the help of many people. And when I graduated, I was the number one chair out of fifty guys in my class. My goal was to work hard enough to get the number one chair, and I did.

It was exciting when I finished school three months early. I really enjoyed learning to be a barber.

I still think about how nice everyone was to me. I learned a lot about life outside the holler, that there were more possibilities than just the mines. I almost stayed in Cincinnati to continue working at the hotel bar because they treated me so well and I made a lot of tips.

After I paid for my train ticket home, I still had $159 saved, which was a lot of money in those days. When I got home, my brother met me at the train station in Princeton, West Virginia. That was the only train station close to the holler.

At home, I got ready to take the West Virginia state board exam in Wheeling so I could start work as a real barber. The day I passed was one of the happiest days of my life, and my mother was very proud of me.

It isn't as easy as you may think to pass the test and get a barber license. You have to do a lot of things besides just cutting hair. You have to take a written test about the body, then you have to do a haircut, shave and massage, while three inspectors check your work.

Finishing barber school took about ten months. After taking the exam, I went to Mullens and started barbering for Ray Davis in his shop by the Five and Dime Store.

There were a lot of pretty girls who worked nearby, and I was the only young barber in town. They all loved to go dancing, which I loved to do, too.

When I got off work on Saturday night, all the people I met on the street complimented me, and it made me feel good.

I couldn't wait to show the people back home that I had finished school. They never thought I would, but I fooled them. I worked hard for all the things I got. Even today, I believe if you work hard, you can do anything, even if other people don't think so.

I have to thank my brother Robert and my mother for helping me get through school. How would you feel if you couldn't bring a friend home because there was no place for them to sleep and my dad might come home drunk? He was mean when he was drunk and would have scared them to death! Mom and Robert's encouragement made all the difference.

After I went to barber college, I didn't see much of my family anymore. We all went our separate ways, except the smallest kids, who moved to Virginia with my mother. We never had much in common because we weren't around one another any more. The last time I saw them was at my mother's funeral.

Bottom line, no matter what your friends might want to do in life, it is important to find what you really want to do. If you do something you love, then every day you will love going to work. If you hate what you do, find something else that you love and you will be successful in your profession.

It's true for both partners in a marriage — if you each love your work, you will be happier, and you'll both have good things to talk about when you are together. It will be good for your family.

I enjoyed getting up and going to work, and I loved every day I was a barber.

Chapter 9

Korean War

Entering the Service

When I got home from barber school, the Korean War was really going strong. I worked as a barber for four or five months and was really happy, but I knew I had to go and serve my country because the military was getting ready to call me in to duty — to draft me.

Instead of waiting to be drafted, I joined the Navy with Joe Dillon, a friend of mine I played baseball with in high school. We picked the Navy because we liked their uniforms! I also wanted to fight for my country, like my brothers did. I was proud to go.

Joe was a good baseball player, and we'd graduated the same year from Mullens High School. We even served on the same ship together after boot training. His parents took us to Princeton, West Virginia, and we enlisted together on April 10, 1952. I served four years, until 1956.

We respected our country, and if there was a war with another country, we were ready to go and proud to serve.

For some men from the holler who didn't want to go to school and were too young to work in the mines, there was nothing else to do but join the military. Families were glad to see you leave because there were usually so many kids still at home.

Plain and simple, it was good to get out of the holler and not have to work in the mines.

I told my brother Jake (Joe), who enlisted before me, that I would see him over there. Jake didn't want to go on to school, so he was only seventeen when he joined the Army. At that age he was really too young to go into the service, but another man signed his papers for him. The man could have gone to jail for that, but my parents decided not to do anything about it.

Jake got killed about ninety days out of boot training when he was blown up in Korea in a tank in the tank battalion. I was in boot training in San Diego when it happened, so I couldn't get leave to go to his funeral. I didn't have the money to go, anyway.

Boot Training

It took us about four days and nights to get to California for our thirteen weeks of boot training. What an experience it was!

Everything was so nice in California, I could hardly believe it. We thought we were going to party when we got there, but boy, did we get fooled!

I will never forget when I saw a chief petty officer for the first time with all those stripes on his arms. I didn't know any better and thought he must be an admiral. The first words out of his mouth were, "Okay, you so-and-so, I don't want to hear another word for thirteen weeks except 'Yes, sir!' and 'No, sir!'"

I was scared, but once we got to the barracks it wasn't that bad — it was better than living in the mountains in West Virginia.

During boot training, I met a lot of nice guys from every part of the country. Some men had never been away from home. I could hear some of them crying at night, so I would go down by the bed and tell them, "Your family is going to be so proud of you when you graduate from boot training."

We couldn't leave boot training until we graduated. The day we graduated, we all looked different — we looked like men.

I finished 40th in my company, out of 117 men. I also made Honor Man in our company. Three of us were nominated, and we went into the restroom while the rest of the company voted.

To get home on leave, we rode a bus four days and four nights.

After training, the men usually didn't see one another again as we all went our separate ways. But we made new friends aboard ship.

The Kearsarge

After training for thirteen weeks, we got liberty. We finally got to party!

When I got back from leave I was assigned to an aircraft carrier, the Kearsarge. The ship was huge, with more than 5,000 men on board.

Once the planes and supplies were all loaded, we headed to Korea. You wouldn't believe how organized we were. We had everything we needed.

Our first stop on the way to Korea was Hawaii. We used to sit in the alleys behind the bar after they closed because we didn't want to go back to the ship until we had to, at 8 in the morning. We could hear the roosters crowing. Hawaii sure has changed from those days. Back then, there was nothing there!

On the second deck of our carrier was where we worked on our planes while we were in action. There were 200 to 300 planes and helicopters on the Kearsarge, and we strapped them down with large cables. No matter how bad the ocean got, everything had to be strapped down or we would have a disaster. The only time we released the planes was when we were in action.

160

I have seen the weather on the ocean so bad that not only did we tie all the airplanes down, we closed all the hatches and stayed below until it blew over. Sometimes the ocean was so bad it would strip back the flight deck, with waves coming over the back half of our deck.

Those ships are all made out of steel and can take any kind of weather. Believe me, they are strong. When the weather out on the ocean got really bad, we did everything we could for our ship and ourselves to survive. That was the way we did things on the ocean. It made us stronger.

Ship's Barber

I knew when I got on that aircraft carrier I was going to find some way to cut hair! I was determined to do it, even if I had to cut hair at night.

They had a large barbershop on the ship, with nice chairs in the crews' barbershop and two barbers in the officers' barbershop.

The way I got to work in the crews' shop was my friend wanted me to cut his hair, so he went to the first officer who was in charge of the crews' shop and had him watch me cut hair. They took my bag to their compartment and he started me in the barbershop right away.

I talked to all the new men I met and treated them nice. A lot of barbers in the service were mean to the men, but not me. When I went down to eat, the guys always wanted me to eat with them. They also invited me into the bars with them, where a lot of the sailors bought me drinks. But if there were other barbers there, they told the bartender the drinks were for me.

I always thought it was better to be nice rather than mean to the other sailors, and I was rewarded for my attitude. They actually used to fly me by helicopter to cut Admiral Hickey's hair on another carrier!

They also had a barber chair in the crew shop where the chief barber cut the leading chief's hair. Even though he was the chief barber, he never took any interest in the type of haircuts the guys wanted or needed.

One day, the lead chief called me outside and asked if I would be their barber. I said yes. When they finished building the barbershop down in the chief's quarters, the chief barber went down as he thought he was supposed to do, but he quickly came right back, yelling, "Wilcox, get your so-and-so down to the chief's shop!"

So I went down and took care of them, and they moved me down to the chief's quarters. I got to eat with them and sleep in their barracks, and they also let me leave the ship with them so I didn't have to stand in line to get off.

Military Order

On the ship we lived according to certain divisions. We never got to know most of the men on the aircraft carrier, but all the men knew their jobs. We worked together, and everybody in each division worked as a team.

The most important thing I learned on the ship was if you treat everyone nice, you'll always be rewarded. I learned that people get along best when they work together in a system. You wouldn't believe how all those men could work together with all those planes in an area that was so big it was like living in a small town. We did a great job on our carrier.

In the military you had your duties and you quickly learned how to do them. Everything in the service has a system, and everyone followed the system. Before we left the States, we had everything in military order and running perfectly!

On an aircraft carrier, there are barracks where the men sleep and relax when they don't have duty or four-hour watches. We stayed clean, including our rooms, because every Friday (or more often, if it was needed) we had an inspection. Everything had better be clean and in order! If it wasn't, we would be put on report, and I didn't want that!

Some men disobeyed and would have to go to the brig where prisoners are confined, or get a dishonorable discharge. I saw a lot of guys who didn't follow their orders, and they didn't get anywhere. They just made it harder on themselves.

We were always on a schedule. There is a certain time to eat each day. We went down to the galley to get our meals and we always stood in line. Actually, we stood in line for just about everything.

We had our watches to stand, but when we had extra time, we played cards and sports activities. When I wasn't on watch or we weren't in action, I cut hair.

A lot of people think that there's nothing to do on an aircraft carrier, but we had movies and all kinds of sports that we competed in with other ships and naval air bases. It kept us busy most of the time.

The guys in our barracks sometimes made life harder than it had to be. There were times they wouldn't want to associate with you or go on liberty with you. Some men loved to start trouble and get in fights at the beach on liberty. Most of us wouldn't hang out with them when they acted that way, especially when they got whipped in a fight! We weren't afraid, but it was better not to fight — though we never ran from anyone if we were right. It was better to have fun on the beach than fight. I had enough of fighting back home, believe me!

Onboard ship, everybody had their problems, as we all do. But you have to live a military life, just like you signed up for, and there are military rules to follow that are very strict. I'm glad they are. That's why we have such a great military.

People don't realize the men in service go through a lot. I could always tell when our buddies got a "Dear John" letter from their wife or girlfriend. Some of them would get mean when there was trouble at home. I learned to stay away from them because that was when we saw a lot of fights. The best thing we could do was let them cool off for a while. Then we tried to make them feel better while they were making up with their wives or girlfriends.

Our aircraft carrier was so big that we had to stay way out at sea because it couldn't get too close to shore. We rowed a boat to shore and back. A lot of the men would party, and there were fights. But when you got back to ship and went aboard, they had the military officers take care of your injuries from fighting. When you are in the military, you are always taken care of.

Everyone worked together as a team and everyone knew where their stations were. For instance, when they rang general quarters, everyone knew what to do. My job was to man a gun to shoot down enemy planes if they came near our ship. When we didn't have to man our guns, we always had other jobs to do, such as work in our living quarters.

But when we weren't at general quarters manning our stations or guns, I cut hair in the crews' barbershop. That sure did help, because I knew I was going to barber when I got out of the service. I got to practice all styles of haircuts and treat the men nice, and they sure appreciated it.

I prepared myself while I was in the service. I did my duty and what I was required to do. And I found out that if you treat people nice, it always comes back to you.

Chapter 10

In Battle

When we were in Korea, we were on battle station call 24 hours a day until we got into a port, and we never saw anything until we got back to port. It didn't matter where we were, we always practiced general quarters so we would know what to do when it was the real thing. We stayed very alert on the ship when we were manning our stations.

I helped manage a five-inch gun when I was on duty. I was the guy who sent the ammunition to the gun. I remember when we were in enemy territory in Korea at general quarters, I was on the five-inch gun and a five-inch shell got stuck inside. Smoke started pouring out of the gun while we were down in the room with all the ammunition — boy, were we scared. One guy ahead of me was trying to get out of there, and I could hardly believe it but he lifted that big steel hatch with his head and was up and out of there. What a relief!

We had three aircraft carriers in our group. The Kearsarge took the center place when we were in action, then they surrounded all the carriers with cruisers, then battleships, and then all the other smaller ships.

We could really perform in battle! That's why I say military life makes a man out of you. You learn how to take care of yourself and your country.

We were in Korea to do a little fighting. The pilots in their planes with bombs or the ones in fighter jets loved to fly and get into the action.

We had hundreds of bombers and fighter planes, 300 pilots and another 5,000 men on the ship. Our planes flew 24 hours a day, around the clock, taking off and landing from a flight deck on top of the ship.

What would scare me the most was when I was standing watch up on the 07 deck, above where the planes came in to land. When they came back from fighting and bombing, sometimes there would be a plane on fire or a bomb that didn't release. That was when I held my breath and prayed that it didn't come loose.

Other times, a plane trying to land would be smoking or had been shot up. We had good firemen on the ship who took care of the ones on fire. All our servicemen were trained to be very professional.

When a plane is in trouble, they have to try and catch it with these large cables that lie across the flight deck. It is very dangerous, especially at night. It seems unbelievable, but a lot of times when the pilots came in from combat with a plane on fire or a bomb stuck, they sent them right back out on another plane. Maybe it was to calm them down.

It was especially scary when a plane trying to take off didn't make it. We put up a big net to try and catch the plane, and the firemen went to work.

On our first trip to Korea, which lasted ten months, we had a lot of losses. Every skipper in every squadron died in battle, along with some of the other pilots who flew with them. That was quite a few.

One time they loaded this pilot's plane to go on a mission, but it was so overloaded he didn't make it into the air and went over the side of the ship. They never did get him out of the plane, even though we had helicopters on each side of the ship. We lost the plane and the pilot.

When someone got killed in action or died at sea, we put him way down in the bottom of the ship in the freezer room. The dead stayed there until we got back to the States or until we arrived in a friendly country for R&R (rest and relaxation) and their bodies could be shipped home.

It got old being stuck on that aircraft carrier out on the ocean with a bunch of men, going through the same routine every day. You learn to deal with it. But it was always nice to get out of the ocean and into port, no matter what country it was.

R&R

No matter what country we were in, it was better than that damp carrier day in and day out. After a little R&R, we were ready to go back out to sea or to the war zone.

When we left Korea for liberty we stopped in quite a few big countries, including Japan, China, Philippines and Mexico, and many smaller countries. Some of those places were brutal and sad — we thanked God we lived in America.

Before we could leave our ship, we had to have a complete inspection. As we went off the ship, the officer of the day (O.D.) stood at the deck where we exited. It was a nice compliment when he said, "You look sharp today, sailor." But there were times the O.D. sent men down below to complete a job before they went on liberty.

The weather in Japan was seasonal, like in California. Thinking back, I can't really remember seeing any fat people there. They were all skinny.

In Japan, we didn't ride in cars or buses — we rode in rickshaws. A rickshaw is a cart with two wheels and a seat, and a Japanese man pulled you around by himself wherever you wanted to go. The rickshaw could only hold two people, and the roads were just little dirt roads and alleys. It was very different compared to riding in a car, but it was fun. I am sure it has changed by now, but that was how it was when I left there in 1952.

In Japan, we could find the most beautiful sets of china dishware, made there or in China. There were dishes, cups and other things, all very professionally made. I sent my mom a nice set.

I was surprised to see such beautiful silk coats and other pieces of clothing. They had pure silk and cashmere. Many service men sent their girlfriends cashmere coats, which were very popular back then. The people who made these things didn't have factories or automation — it was all done by hand.

The Japanese were the neatest, cleanest people I ever saw, considering what little they had. There were silk shops downstairs and girls upstairs, all wearing fancy evening gowns. They were great at giving massages — they could crack your bones and make you relax.

One year, we were in Yokosuka, Japan, on my birthday. My buddy Uffer and I were standing outside this dance place waiting for some friends to take me to my birthday party. As we stood waiting in the alley, it was raining real hard and we had our pea coats over our heads, trying to stay as dry as we could. Someone pecked me on the shoulder, and I turned around to find two big guys in civilian clothes. One of them said, "I asked my friend, 'Do you want to go into the dance hall or do you want to whip those two sailors?'" Then he said, "My friend doesn't want to go into the dance hall!"

By this time, Uffer had taken off down the alley, calling for me to come. I decided I wasn't leaving, so I told the guy, "If you want to fight us, why don't you let your friend watch you and me fight?" They agreed.

But when I took my neckerchief off and we started fighting, the other guy jumped in on me, too. When the people standing around saw that, they stopped the fight. I was so muddy you could hardly recognize me. I went inside to get a drink and when I tossed my head back to drink, I realized my two front teeth were knocked out.

The funny part was, the next morning when I went back to the ship, the officer of the deck didn't know who I was because I was still covered with mud. Boy, did he chew me out.

Even though we were away from the ship and there wasn't a whole lot to do on liberty in Yokosuka, we still stayed out on liberty until the last minute before going back. But if a sailor didn't return to the ship every day, he would be put on report.

When we went to Hong Kong, China, I think the conditions were pretty close to how most Chinese people lived. The people were very poor, but the country was very clean.

Right across from Hong Kong there were border countries. Across the ocean on one side was Kowloon, less than a mile from us. It was off limits, but sometimes when we were in Hong Kong we would go over just to see what was there, which turned out to be nothing. But we were curious so we had to look.

We also went to the Philippine islands and to Mexico. Both countries were very poor back then.

The people we saw in the Philippines had a different way of living compared to the Japanese and Chinese people. A lot different. The Filipino people we saw were not as neat and clean as the Japanese and Chinese. They believed in barbecuing dogs and cats for food. It was my observation that if you had dealings with them, they would cheat you, and maybe even get your dog and barbecue it!

We also crossed the equator. Everyone had to go through an initiation if it was our first time to cross, and we received a certificate saying we had crossed it.

When you go overseas and see how people live, you feel great about our country and all that we have in comparison.

The service took me to Japan, China, Subic Bay and Manila in the Philippines, Korea, Singapore, Mexico, Hong Kong, Kowloon, across the equator, and all the other countries. But nothing compares to the good old USA. Ours is the best country in the world!

When you get home from military duty, you are a different person. It's not about going to war with other countries, it is how the military trains these young men, and when they get home they appreciate everything we have in our country. I know, because I saw it all happen. That is why we need military training, because when our kids get out, they will be proud of themselves and know right from wrong.

On Leave

When we came back to the states, either to our own base or another station, such as Long Beach or San Francisco, we had thousands of people there to welcome us, including some of the men's families. It was quite a celebration.

But no matter what place you landed, you still had your station to man. The way the military worked was if you had your family waiting for you at the dry dock, someone else would stand by for you, especially if their family and friends had traveled from another state. But if you didn't have someone, you would have to stand your own duty. Most of the time, if someone's family was out on the dock to meet the ship, we would stand by for them. They really appreciated that because many families lived on the East Coast.

A lot of times I didn't have money to take leave, so I stayed on ship. Sometimes we got invited to a buddy's home for the weekend. It was a treat to get off the ship in California and go somewhere. That was how I found out about Newman and Gustine in the San Joaquin Valley. What great little towns, and the people were very nice. The lifestyle in California was completely different compared to where I grew up. But just like in West Virginia, they were very hardworking people.

I used to take my leave in Newman and stay with the families of fellows I served with. While I was there, Bob Gaddy let me work for him at the tire shop so I could make some spending money, and we would go out every night. When it was time to go back to the ship, I hitchhiked. When you had a service uniform on, it was easy to get a ride. Sometimes people even took you right to your ship.

Honorable Discharge

When we served, we came back changed men.

The first two trips to Korea were okay, but the final one seemed to last forever. Even so, I was still proud to have served our country. Just stop and think, I would never have found out what a great state California is, with its wonderful weather, the great people of all nationalities and all the ways a person can become successful.

We were so restricted in what we could do on the aircraft carrier that I couldn't wait to get off. It was sure nice to get back on U.S. soil and let someone else take over for a change.

I knew I didn't have much more time in the service and I wasn't about to sign up again. Military life wasn't my thing. I was looking forward to getting out and starting life.

I had been on the ship for forty months when the leading chief of fighter attack squadron V.F. 112 asked me if I would cut commander Piller's hair.

I said, "Sure! He likes flattops, and I can do that."

Before long, the chief asked me how I would like to move into the V.F. 112 squadron.

I said, "Everybody promises that when we're in the States."

About two weeks later, he came down to the shop and said, "Darrell, you're now in the V.F. 112. Here are your papers."

I was never so happy in all my life!

I went to Miramar Air Station in San Diego with my squadron. When we got in our barracks, everybody welcomed us. I worked there until I was discharged.

You wouldn't believe the difference between being on the ship and being stationed at Miramar. When you live on a ship, you stay on that ship unless you are going on liberty or business, and then you have a certain time to be back on the ship or you will be put on report. That's why I was so glad to get off the ship and get on land.

When I got my discharge and left the carrier, I still cut hair in the barracks, and everyone treated me well.

When I cut their hair, I sat the fellows on a garbage can for a barber chair! Sometimes I made a little money to go on liberty. If they didn't have any money, I cut it for free, practicing different types of haircuts. Barbers don't just cut hair, they have to shape the style to a person's face. A little thing like that means a lot to people on base.

My first job was to sweep the barracks twice a day, and then we got to go to town at 5 p.m.

I stayed at Miramar Air Station the last eight months before I was discharged. It was a treat to cut the commander's and the leading chief's hair every week.

One time before my leave was about to start, I kept calling home for Mom to send my money for a plane ticket home.

She never said a thing until my leave started, then she said, "Darrell, I had to spend your money."

So with all my money gone, I told a friend of mine what happened. When we got back on the ship, he went to the guys in the squadron and they gave me $138. I just hitchhiked home from San Diego — it took four days and four nights without much sleep.

When I got home, there was only $158 left in the bank, which I used to buy a bus ticket back to San Diego when my leave was over. I had sent home $2,400 — that was a lot of money back then! But I wasn't mean to my mother; I knew who had really spent the money, and it wasn't my mother. But if she needed my money, God bless her.

The thing that made me mad was that she didn't tell me until the day my leave was starting. Thank God, I treated the sailors in my squadron well or they wouldn't have given the $138 to help me out.

Back at Miramar, finishing up my time in the service and waiting to get discharged, I met a lot of people on base. One day I got a surprise from the head of the Chiefs' Club at Miramar. He wanted to meet me because the chief at V.F. 112 squadron told him about me cutting hair. He gave me a job at the Chiefs' Club to help with parties and to cut his hair, which I did. That was a lot of fun. They had a lot of parties there, and I really enjoyed it. I treated them the same way I treated the guys on the ship.

He was a pretty nice guy. He owned a baby blue Cadillac and he sometimes loaned it to me to go to San Diego in the evenings on liberty. It was fun! But as nice as that great big car was, I just didn't feel comfortable driving it.

On the last day in the Navy before I came home, a guy I played baseball with propositioned me. I was so dumbfounded that I locked him out of my room and told him I was going to call the cops. I had never seen anything like that before, except maybe a few people in Mullens. We never paid any attention to them back then because they never bothered us. I learned a lot about people and the world when I was in the Navy. What an experience!

While I was in the service I had met a wonderful young woman, Dorothy Lloyd from Gustine, because I worked with her Uncle Harlan. He introduced us.

After we'd been going out for quite a while, I took my buddy John Drew to go pick out an engagement ring for her in San Diego. John was a small guy, and would you believe I used his finger to fit the ring? It worked perfectly!

Unfortunately, on our way back from San Diego, we wrecked the car (not the Cadillac). John was driving. Thank God, no one was hurt, but the car was torn up.

When I asked Dorothy to marry me, we were going down Highway 140 near Gustine, and she accepted. There was only one thing that I asked her to do, and she agreed with me — we promised we would not fight and argue, especially in the morning, because we had both lived through that at home. It's a promise we always kept.

When I got my discharge, I was so proud it was an honorable discharge and not anything less. I left the service March 23, 1956, and had earned the National Defense Service Medal, China Service Medal, Korean Service Medal (Two Stars), and the United Nations Service Medal. After that, I was considered to be on Inactive Duty until my final discharge April 9, 1960.

The chief even gave me a great big party. I was one happy man as I headed north to get married in Gustine, where my sweetheart lived!

Chapter 11

Civilian Life and Marriage

Gustine was Dorothy's hometown, and it was there that we started planning our wedding.

I wanted to get married quickly because I couldn't wait to get home to barber in Mullens, but I needed to make some extra money to get us back to West Virginia. My barber's license was only good in West Virginia, you see.

While we were preparing for the wedding, I went back to work at Bob Gaddy's tire shop. He treated me well.

Bob used to say, "I want my boy, Bob Junior, to have everything he wants, because when I was growing up I never got to have those things."

But by giving his boy so much, Bob Junior grew up, became a bum and died on the streets from alcoholism at 47 years old.

I think we owe our kids better than that. People who think they have to give them everything they want and never make them work for it soon learn that the kids never appreciate it. It all starts with the family. When children are born, the biggest mistake we can make is never teaching them the value of working for what they want in life. It's good for kids to appreciate their parents and work for what they get.

During this time I also worked in a rose garden where Ray Retiez gave me a job. I didn't know how to drive a tractor and I wound up tearing down half his roses.

Dorothy and I finally got married in Gustine. It was a small ceremony in the Baptist church, with Dorothy's family and friends present. My best man was Dorothy's Uncle Harlan.

Back to West Virginia

As soon as the wedding was over, I bought a car and we headed to West Virginia. We were so in love and didn't have a care in the world.

This was my first car, and I was about 23 years old.

The first place we stopped was at my mother's in Virginia. It hadn't changed one bit.

When we got to Mullens, we rented a one-bedroom apartment behind a friend's house.

One day, my mother took Dorothy up above the coal camp holler to the cabin where my dad lived. When they got next to the cabin, he started throwing rocks at them.

Dorothy said, "He sure scared me and your mother! We ran to the car and got out of there."

Things had been pretty bad for my mother until she moved to Virginia with all the kids. Every weekend I couldn't help but think about how bad the weekends were when I was young. I tried to think about something else, like living in California someday. There's no comparison between California and West Virginia. I knew that if I worked hard there, I could get ahead.

I proved to a lot of people back home that I would return as a barber. I knew how to do any kind of haircut after being in the service, and I couldn't wait to show them what I could do.

I went back to work at Ray Davis' barbershop in Mullens. It was tough at first because I was in the back on the fourth chair, and nobody really knew me. But when they saw I could cut all types of hair and perform other services, my business really grew.

I'm not bragging — I was a good barber and I loved the competition. Pretty soon I had a lot of people waiting for me, especially for flattops that were popular. I was an expert at them. To make extra money I shot pool and played poker.

I remember Willie Atkins' dad was a railroad boss. When I was barbering in West Virginia, Willie played basketball for West Virginia University. That's also how I met Jerry West, the famous basketball player. At that time, Jerry played for West Virginia University with Willie. Jerry would come up and visit Willie sometimes and play summer basketball, and they would come into the barbershop to shoot some bull.

One year, Mullens High School played East Bank High School for the championship. East Bank was where Jerry West had gone to school. His team beat us by one point. He scored 41 points that night, and for one week the town of East Bank changed their name to West Bank. Jerry was such a nice boy, a real fine gentleman, and so was Willie Atkins. I also knew Rod Thorn, a pro basketball player, and another pro player who was called "Hot Rod" Huntley.

Dorothy and I stayed in West Virginia, and I made a good living. Our first child, Darla, was born nine months and nine days after we were married. I bet everybody in town the baby was going to be a boy.

After she was born I asked the nurse, "Are you sure it's a girl?"

She brought Darla up to the window and took her diaper down. That nurse made a believer out of me.

We had a friend in the holler, Don Needle, who worked in a funeral home and embalmed people. I often went with him to pick up people who died and miners who were killed. We brought them into the funeral home, where I helped embalm them and get them ready for the viewing and burial. I was always amazed at how nice he treated them — very respectfully, just like they were alive.

When Dorothy and I returned to West Virginia for visits after we moved away, I always helped Don at the funeral home.

Back then, people visited each other more than they do today. On weekends, everyone got together by the woodsheds to play cards, pitch horseshoes and play all kinds of games. There were even a lot of good marble shooters.

One night, Don and I went to a basketball tournament in Pineville where the team from Mullens was playing. When we came back to Mullens, we stopped at the Eat Well Cafe, where people liked to go at night. I played the jukebox, listened to music and had a cold one. We were sitting in the back.

I put some quarters on the bar and left for a minute. When I came back to sit down, Don told me that a guy in the booth got my quarters and put them in the jukebox. I went over and nicely asked him about my quarters, and he sort of pushed me back all of a sudden. Without thinking, I saw a Coca-Cola case by me, so I picked it up and beat him over the head with it.

They pulled me off of him, and then the cops and ambulance came. The snow was real deep as the cops were taking me to the car, so I took off running and they couldn't catch me.

On Monday morning, I went to see the police chief and told him what happened. I said, "If you'll wait till the snow gets off the ground, I'm going back to California."

He replied, "I'll wait till the snow gets off the ground, and you better be gone."

So when the snow had all melted, Dorothy and I packed our car and left West Virginia, as I promised. We never had any problems along the way, except Darla wanted to stop every few minutes to go potty. I bought her a potty chair and we continued on our way.

The day we pulled into my in-laws' driveway, I felt right at home. We had been in West Virginia for four years, but I had always thought about California. You couldn't pay me to go back in those hills now.

Today, there still isn't anything in Mullens. It's a very depressed area.

I never regretted coming back to California. It took about four years to make it, but we did. There were so many more opportunities in California than in West Virginia. I never looked back.

Before we moved, Dorothy said she did not want to go back to California because she liked the people in Mullens and loved her church. She was also concerned

I might not like living there. She said, "don't blame me if you don't like California."

But she soon saw how happy I was. Our arrival also thrilled her mother and father. It was great for Dorothy and Darla to be close to them.

Part 5

CALIFORNIA

Chapter 12

Settling in Newman

When I got out of the service and we went back to West Virginia, I still thought about California. So when we came back, I felt right at home. There is no comparison. When you have never been out of West Virginia, it is hard to understand how different it is to live way out west.

Most people in West Virginia have never known anything else, so I can't blame them for staying there. If I had not gone into the service and been stationed in California, I probably would have felt the same way and still be living back east.

When I first saw California, I couldn't believe how nice it was. The weather is beautiful all year-round. If we want snow, we drive to it, and when we get tired of it, we come back down to the San Joaquin Valley. When it is cold, raining and snowing in West Virginia, the sun is usually shining in California, and there is always something to do.

Here, we have the greatest farmers and dairies in the world, and some of the largest orchards and grape vineyards on earth.

License to Barber

Since my goal was to work as a barber in California, I quickly enrolled in barber school in Stockton so I could get my California barber license. As soon as I finished, I took my state license test in San Francisco and passed. I started looking around Newman for a place to put my shop.

I always thought about setting up my shop in Newman because the people were so nice to me when I visited while on leave.

I started my shop with three dollars. As soon as I found out I could buy barbershop equipment and make monthly payments on it, I was on my way. Our house rent was forty dollars a month and the shop rent was fifty dollars a month.

Newman was a town of about 3,000 people, and it already had three barbers. That didn't bother me. I would go and cut people's hair when they were in the hospital or in their homes when they were sick, and I began building a good reputation. I got acquainted with everybody and I loved to talk about sports. It was to my benefit that none of the other barbers talked about sports.

I was proud of my barbershop. The whole time I worked there I never took time out for lunch or had a telephone in the shop. I was serious about my work and loved it so much I didn't want any distractions.

Jesse Vella, a good friend who would have died for me, used to bring food to me at the barbershop, but I was too busy to eat it until I got home. He also taught me about black bass fishing.

God blessed me and my family. The shop was making money, so I surprised Dorothy by buying a lot in Newman to build a house on. I knew that women love to design their own floor plans. I told her to build the house any way she wanted.

It is important to a woman how the home is laid out. Men don't understand. In those days, men usually didn't do the cleaning and were at work most of the time.

My wife and the contractor did a beautiful job building our house. She was happy and she never heard any complaints from me.

Portuguese Friends

We worked hard all week, and it was good to get together and visit with our Portuguese friends on weekends. We had parties in one another's homes and went to dances and Portuguese celebrations. We danced the Chamarita at their big dinner dances in different clubs. Everyone got along well.

They were known for cooking huge amounts of good homemade food in their big pots, and they let me help. It was delicious! They would take me to their homes and show me how to make their favorite recipes, such as Portuguese beans (with beans grown in my own garden), homemade sausage, blood sausage, linguica (seasoned pork sausage), and favish, a dish made with fava beans.

Portuguese and Italian friends made wine when the grapes got ripe, and we all sampled it. The Okies, like me, made home-brew.

Back then, everybody worked. We never heard of food stamps, or things like that. The Portuguese people always work hard and are very honest and trusting. But if they found you were crooked, they had nothing more to do with you.

Every Wednesday and Friday night we went to Ben's Club to watch the boxing matches with the Salano brothers, Andy Correia, and a lot of others. We bet on the fights and there was never an issue among any of us about a wager. My friends also introduced me to auctions and boxing matches in Stockton.

I could speak Portuguese very well when I was in the barbershop, and I learned Spanish, too. I became great friends with Mexican people.

At that time, the farm workers lived in labor camps. They were very nice. One of the workers would come into the shop and let me know a group of them was coming in for haircuts, so I got them a case of beer and some girlie magazines. I learned a lot about how they lived.

Most of the other people I met in the barbershop were what I called Okies, and I was one of them. They were great people, too.

Local Church

My family attended church in Newman. When we saw that there was no carpet on the floor and Pastor Voss didn't have any furnishings in the pulpit, Harold Canter and I went to the board of the church to see why.

They told us they didn't have any money.

We asked, "What if the congregation votes to buy what the church needs?"

The board said, "If you go and ask all the members, and if they vote on it, we will do it."

So Harold and I went door to door. The night of the vote, the church was full, and everyone voted for everything we needed.

You should have seen what a beautiful church we had after we were done. Our pastor was so excited.

We even put up new advertising signs out on Highway 33. I really have to thank Harold Canter for all his help.

A lot of preachers run their churches like a chief, but not Pastor Voss. He was also a schoolteacher. He and his wonderful wife had four children.

I learned all of my religion from Dorothy. I never attended church until after we were married.

But to be totally truthful, on my days off I played golf while she took the kids to church.

Dorothy was a great Christian. Even when we were in West Virginia, she always went to church on Sunday.

And when we lived in Newman, she brought the kids to the golf course after church so they could go swimming.

On Sunday, I was a regular at the golf course. But if the church needed anything, I was always there to help.

In Wyco holler, no one ever told me about going to church or about the Lord Jesus Christ. But when I met Dorothy, she led me to accept Jesus Christ as my savior, and I was baptized in California.

For such a small town, we had a lot of clubs and churches there.

Lions Club

One club I joined was the Lions Club, and soon I became president. We had a huge Easter breakfast fundraiser and made more money that year than the club had ever raised before.

I was voted Lions Club chairman for the San Joaquin Valley, but I was so busy I asked Johnny Oliveria to take my place. He was one of the best workers in the club. Also helping our town were Harold Canter and Bill Burnette — nobody worked harder and got less credit than these men.

While we were living in Newman, I helped put on the first junior rodeo. Even though I had never ridden a horse in my life, I decided to ride a bull if people made a donation to the Meza family, who had some family members killed in a car wreck. We had about 5,000 people there. They took up a good donation for the family, so I did what I said — I rode a bull! I didn't stay on long because it threw me off and sort of knocked me out. I had to go to the hospital, but it was worth it. We raised a lot of money, but I won't ride any more bulls, that's for sure.

Some of the best times I can remember were with local coaches. We had a lot of fun being active in sports. We went to all the ball games, and the fellowship was great.

Dorothy and I often saw many friends and acquaintances at parties and ball games.

Bookie Joint

Speaking of sports, I operated a bookie joint in my barbershop in Newman where we bet on ball games and boxing matches. We bet on everything, in fact.

At that time, the fights in the east were broadcast three hours before they aired on television here in the west because of the time difference. I would call back east, and they would tell me who won, so I knew ahead of time who to bet on. That was easy money.

Frank Silva and I bet on the second fight for the heavyweight championship between Cassius Clay and Sonny Liston, in May of 1965. I won enough money on that fight to fly back to West Virginia for a visit. I heard later that Frank told Joe Anthony, "I hope that plane blows up." Frank and I were really great friends, but very competitive. We just loved to beat each other at whatever we did.

When a pool hustler came to town, I always met him after work. One time, Doug Stephens and his friend brought in a pool hustler they knew from Santa Rosa. After I got through with work, I went over to the Rose Hotel Bar, got his money and sent him back to Santa Rosa.

Besides pool, we played poker for money. We had a few tricks with our partners. When we brought a new person into the game, we gave one another signals, such as lighting a cigarette or asking a certain question. That told us what the other guy had in his hand. But no matter what, we didn't want to get caught. And if we did get caught, we had to run — fast! Sometimes with certain guys in the game I was too scared to cheat.

I wouldn't lie in any of my business dealings, but back then, if I played golf, poker or pool with you, it was "every man for himself." I guess I felt that way because in the holler, survival often meant taking advantage of every opportunity, even if it wasn't exactly the right thing to do.

In gambling, you find people who think they are the greatest at it. They think they know everything, but they don't really know anything. That is called ego.

I like competition. It makes you excel. But I have seen some great athletes who choke when you bet a lot of money on them.

The biggest thing in any sport or game is this: If you can't stand the pressure then you shouldn't be playing, so don't bet money in the first place. A lot of people just love to bet. Even though they know they are probably going to lose, they will play, and choke every time. But they still have to pay the money even if they lose.

Family Businesses

I went into all of my businesses with my wife and kids helping me. I couldn't have made it if it weren't for them. Thank God, I had my family to help me. It was a lot of hard work, but it was fun, too.

Dorothy and I had good times together when our children were growing up. Sometimes, though, when the weekends came, I would think about how I grew up with so much yelling, arguing and fighting. That is why we didn't have any fighting and arguing in our house.

We also didn't believe in spoiling our kids. They were taught to mind their parents, unlike a lot of families today where the kids don't mind and they are handed everything they want without ever learning to work for it.

Responsibility should come early. Even before my kids were in high school they could run any of our businesses. If my wife and I didn't have their help, I'm not sure what we would have done. Maybe I am bragging, but I am proud of the way that they stepped up and helped.

You should always do what you love and enjoy your work, because if you hate what you do every day, it's not fun. Find what you love to do and you will succeed.

Also, keep in mind that when you build a business, someone always wants to buy it. With my donut shop, I had about 23 outlets in three small towns selling our donuts. The minute I was ready to sell the business, someone was ready to buy it.

The way to be successful is by being honest and working hard. When I got one business built up, that's when I started another business. When I got through, I had about eleven or twelve businesses at one time.

I loved every day I worked as a barber, but when I got tired of it after about thirty years, I closed and locked my door in Newman and walked away.

Newman was where I got my start in business, and I'll always remember it as a wonderful place. The people were great to me, like one big family. Everybody worked hard, and we had a lot of fun.

Chapter 13

Branching Out

Gustine

We were very busy in Newman and Gustine, operating two beauty shops, a children's store and the barbershop. Not to brag, but my family and I never went broke in any of our businesses.

I started building businesses kind of by accident when a man named Melvyn Souza asked, "Why don't you build my wife a beauty shop in Gustine?"

Pat Souza was nice and had the best personality in Newman. She was also the hardest-working person I had ever seen. She started every morning at 5:30 and worked until about 9 at night.

I built the beauty shop in Gustine, and she named it Pat's House of Beauty. The shop had five beauty operator stations. She ran four other beauty shops, so we did real well working with the Souzas. Even to this day, she is still a hard worker and has a great husband who helps her.

Rose Costa owned a beauty shop, too. When her husband got transferred to a bigger city, I bought her shop and called it Magic Mirror. Guess who washed all the towels in that beauty shop? It was me and my kids. And when we got through washing towels, the kids were so fast they could beat me folding them up.

Later on I opened a children's store for Dorothy in Gustine. Dorothy and Darla designed the store and bought the clothes, and Dorothy ran it. She named the store Kiddie Corner, and everyone in Gustine became our customers. They were very good to us.

Stevenson

Most of the people who lived in Stevenson were what I call Okies, like me. When the interest rates went up to about 18 to 22 percent, I sold a lot of owner-financed property. I got acquainted with the people at Stevenson Bar and Grill because a lot of people hung out there, and they gave me tips on who was selling their property. I bought them a beer for the lead.

When I became a property owner, I bought five houses in Stevenson and became a landlord. The biggest problem I had was when it came time to collect the rent. My renters were either out of the house or had some kind of excuse why they couldn't pay.

One of my renters kept lying to me and making excuses why they didn't have the rent. One day when I went to collect, I discovered they had moved out in the night and left the house a mess. The lady down the road told me they moved to Hilmar, which was not too far away. I got my friend's truck and hauled all the junk and trash they left behind to Hilmar. When I pulled up and started unloading all the junk, his wife came out and started yelling at me. I just threw it all over their yard and told her, "That's the way you left my house!"

There were a lot of great people in Stevenson. One couple named Frank and Mary Silva owned a store there for about forty years or more. When I handled the real estate listing and sold it for them, we became very good friends.

I also met two guys from San Jose who built homes in the area, and sold them a lot of property. There was one thing I could never figure out about them, though. They were smart, successful businessmen and they worked hard every day. But at 5 o'clock, they would start drinking until they passed out. Somehow, they were always able to work the next day. I liked them, but I never figured out why they did that. It just didn't make sense to me. They were both good in business, but they died from their drinking. I sure learned a lot from them in regard to building homes and subdivisions, and I used to acquire all their land for them.

In Stevenson, the best time to make money was at night on the weekends, because a lot of people from the San Jose area came around to shoot pool and drink beer. I would buy them a beer, and then the whole table bought more beer. When they went to the bathroom after all that drinking, I spit on their pool cue tip, which made it slippery when it hit the ball.

That is called pool hustling. Let me be clear — all my business deals were always honest. But when you get on the pool table or any other sport, I worked it to my advantage, and I don't regret it.

The town of Stevenson is still there and it's still the same — it hasn't grown one bit. It is still just a store, gas station and beer joint, and that's it.

I still drive through that little town every time I play golf in Turlock.

Oakdale

It wasn't long until I went to Oakdale and bought another pizza parlor. Oakdale was cowboy country USA. It was so beautiful up in the hills I almost decided to move there.

About this time, Darla wanted a car, so I took her to Modesto to look at some. We stopped at a used car lot, and she started crying.

I said, "Darla, what is wrong with you?"

She said, "Dad, you promised me a new car."

She had been working hard, and I had to admit she deserved a new car, so that is what she got.

The most money I ever made at one time was in Oakdale. Gordie Rose, who bought and sold cattle, bet me $33,000 or his meat plant, House of Beef, in a game of pool. I won, but I didn't take anything because we were good friends and he had a nice wife and four little girls to take care of. Also, I may have helped him lose by spitting on his pool stick when he was in the bathroom and making sure he had plenty of beer. He had $700 on him and he gave that to me. But it was two days before Christmas, so I gave him back $400 so he could take his family to San Bernardino for the holiday.

One day when I was in the pizza parlor and everyone else was gone, two cowboys came in. One said, "Don't get scared if we come riding in on our horses."

The pizza parlor had big swinging doors in the front, big enough for two horses and riders. They got through the doors, all right, so I went into the dough room and came out with my double-barreled shotgun. I said, "I've got a shell for each horse!"

You should have seen the look on their faces when I pointed that shotgun at them! They got the message real quick!

In Oakdale, I got to know Harley May, the world champion bull rider; the Camarilla family, who were the team roping champions; and Kenny Roberts, the motorcycle world champion.

It was in Oakdale that I first started working to get my real estate license. I knew a realtor named Red Avila who bet me $50 that I wouldn't go to Fresno and take the real estate license test.

I took that bet and went and took the test. I flunked it, but I made $50. After that, I went to real estate school in Modesto and eventually passed the test.

Dorothy was a brilliant business lady. She had a great personality and everybody liked her. With all the businesses we were buying and building, we were excited to get our real estate license.

When I decided to learn how to make donuts, I made a deal with a guy in Modesto to show him how to make pizzas if he would show me how to make donuts. I used to drive to Modesto every day until I learned to make every kind of donut. It was hard work, and hot work. You do everything by minutes and seconds or you don't have a good product. After the guy started making pizzas with me, he decided he didn't like it.

It was exciting getting into new businesses. We learned a lot of things. There was always someone to show us a new skill, and we could teach them in exchange.

Firebaugh

Looking to open another business, Dorothy and I went to a little town up the road called Firebaugh. We poked around and saw that they didn't have any donut shops in the three-town area of Dos Palos, Firebaugh and Mendota.

We built the donut shop, basing the kitchen in Firebaugh because it was in the middle of the three towns. One town was nine miles away and the other was fourteen miles away.

We were the only shop offering donuts in the whole area, with 23 outlets in the three towns. We did very well. People loved our donuts, and they were nice to support us.

My workday started at midnight, and I didn't come home until after I got through making the donuts and getting them out. I had one of the nicest girls working for me, Suzie Sugam, who delivered the donuts to each of the towns and also helped me in the shop.

We had a lot of fun working in the early morning as all the farmers stopped by on their way to work. The farmers told some good stories and jokes while I made the donuts.

Going home after making the donuts, I was so tired I had to stop on the way to Los Banos and pour water over my head so I wouldn't fall asleep driving. One morning, a lady came out of her house and wanted to know if I was all right.

I told her, "I worked half the night and got sleepy driving, so I stopped to get some cold water out of the canal to wake me up."

From then on, when I stopped at the canal by her house, I gave her some donuts.

In Firebaugh, they had a cantaloupe festival every year, and it brought in a lot of people. At that time, picking cantaloupes was hard work. Workers picked the cantaloupes by hand and hauled them to a packing shed where other people boxed them. Sometimes you could go to the sheds and buy them before they put them in the boxes. Today, it is still hard work, and they still pick by hand, but they box them right in the fields. They don't need packing sheds anymore.

It is the same way with a lot of the crops these days — everything is done right in the fields. That wasn't how it was done when I was raised. And the dairy business has also changed a lot since I was young — no more milking the cows by hand.

The San Joaquin Valley is the greatest farming country in the world. Thank God for our farmers. I wish someone would tell me today why some of these idiots don't want our farmers to have all the water they need. Their farms are what feed our country and make plenty of jobs for our people. Some people, like politicians and environmentalists, just don't understand that we should be proud of our farmers and dairymen. They would rather try and save some stupid, good-for-nothing little animal than our farms and dairy businesses.

Chapter 14

Los Banos

Dorothy and I had things going on all over. In Oakdale we had a pizza parlor; in Firebaugh, a donut shop; and donut outlets in Dos Palos and Mendota.

We still lived in Newman for a while after we opened the store in Los Banos. We decided to move to Los Banos because we had more things going on there than in Gustine, about twenty miles away. Our businesses included a pizza parlor, Mexican restaurant, steak house, children's store, ladies' dress shop, real estate office and a gravel business.

We loved selling real estate, and Dorothy was a great salesperson. She knew everybody in town and they all liked her.

In Los Banos, I was the first realtor to work on Saturday and Sunday. I was so busy that soon everyone in the Century 21 office wanted to work weekends. It turned out to be very good for everybody.

Scotty Henderson, the broker I worked with, said, "Darrell, let's split up so we can take turns working Saturday and Sunday because that is the busiest time of the week."

That gave me time to spend with the family and prepare for our move.

Our three wonderful children were quickly growing up. I thought Darla, Darrell Junior, and Kim would get mad when we moved, but they accepted it, and before you know it they made friends. The only reason we didn't move from Newman sooner was so Darla could graduate from high school. After we moved, Darrell Junior started high school (ninth grade), and Kim started seventh grade.

While we were in Newman, Darrell's baseball team won the championship in a game in which he hit a grand slam home run. It was no surprise that when Darrell reached high school, he was a good athlete in all sports.

As for me, I kept up with my pool playing. One night when I was in Danny's bar in Los Banos, there was a hotshot pool player there. I watched him shoot, and I told all the onlookers that I would play him one-handed. Everybody took bets, and as I recall, Tony Labe and Aldo Sansoni were there. I think there was about $100 in bets, maybe more.

I went out to my car, got my big shoe brush, carefully laid it down upside down while they all watched, and took my shot one-handed. I did very well and won the money.

There is one thing you have to know when you're a pool hustler, and that's how to play a player. If he shoots fast, you shoot slow. And when he goes to the bathroom or is talking to someone, wherever he leaves his stick, I'm always right beside it. Why? So I can spit on the pool cue tip. There is no way he can shoot with a wet tip.

When there is money involved, it is pressure, pressure, pressure. Most people shoot great when there is no money involved. I used to get on a pool table and lose four or five games on purpose. Of course, they wanted to bet money against me then. I loved it, because when money was involved, I didn't lose.

That is called hustling.

Golf

Besides being a barber, I had another dream: I wanted to be a professional golfer. I never got that far, but I became a very good player.

I saw my first golf course in Princeton, West Virginia. I was about 24 years old and excited to play golf for the first time. I probably shot a 200.

I really never knew anything about golf, so the way I started playing was by going golfing with Bill Turner from Newman, Dale Lowry and Gerald Hunt. They were all good players, but the one who amazed me the most was Bill Turner — what a golfer!

The night after that first golf game I went to Bill's apartment, right across the street from my barbershop, and asked him if he could teach me how to hit the ball. Bill was a retired colonel and a schoolteacher, and he wore a white Ben Hogan hat. When I saw how great he was, I knocked on his door. He answered it wearing the hat.

I asked, "Bill, how much would you charge me to teach me some golf out in the football field?"

The price was reasonable, and I got him to teach me a lot about golf. With his help and after a year of hard work, mostly at night, I shot 79 the first time I played at Dryden Park Golf Course in Modesto. It was one of my biggest thrills, and that was my first year playing golf!

Then at Turlock Golf and Country Club, I had a hole in one at the ninth hole when it was a par 3. It was on a Sunday, and Dale Lowry, Gerald Hunt and Darrell Junior were with me. I was glad there weren't very many people in the clubhouse because I had to buy everybody a drink.

Maybe the reason I improved so fast was because we always played for money.

We used to have so much fun at the country club parties and swimming in the summer. Our pro, George Buzzini

Sr., was one of the hardest-working pros around the clubhouse and one of the best competitors I ever saw.

It's true that any sport you really love, forget the others and work hard on the one.

I remember as if it were yesterday — I was in the kitchen in my restaurant in Los Banos and my son came in very serious and said, "Dad, can I talk to you? You know, Dad, I want to be the best golfer on the high school team."

I looked at him and said, "Darrell, you know when we practice, it's all business. Tell me what you want to do."

"I want to work hard on my golf," he said. "And I promise to practice."

And he did. He was already one heck of a baseball and football player, so I knew he would apply himself just as seriously to golf.

We agreed on a plan, and guess what! Not only did he work hard, he won all the competitions in Northern California. It was wonderful to watch him do all this while he was still in high school.

He won the individual player award with two under 70 in Sacramento, at Rancho Murrieta. No one from Merced County had ever won that individually — you can check the records. As a high school senior competing against all the college kids, he won the

Stockton City Tournament with an eight under par. Nobody in Merced County ever did that. He even asked me to caddy for him. That tickled me!

When he played, he never showed any emotion, but boy, could he play under pressure. Dorothy and Darrell Junior's friends Paul Enos and John Test were up there with us, and they were more excited than Darrell was. Other good friends he ran around with were Rick Howard and John Santos. All these boys were great kids.

While he was playing, and after the tournament was over, he talked to me about what he should work on to make his game better. He thought about going to see a professional golfer. He got great advice from George Buzzini Sr. But, honestly, our greatest teacher was Bill Turner. He was the best.

So you see, even as a child, working hard pays off.

When Darrell Junior was playing golf in the Stockton City Tournament, there was a lady following him around on the putting green.

I asked him, "What does that lady want?"

Darrell said, "She wants me to model clothes for her company, but I told her, 'No way! I'm not a sissy!'"

We never mentioned it again. But as time went on, I would think about how funny it was, from bucking hay to modeling clothes.

When he wanted to buck hay, he dressed nice and went to Meneze Brothers to see if he could get a job, but they sent him home. I called them and asked why they didn't give my boy a chance to buck hay for them. They found out that Darrell was best friends with Pat Meneze, so they asked him to come back and said they would give him a chance, and they hired him.

John Meneze was the hardest-working man in the San Joaquin Valley. Whenever I cut his hair, he had one foot on the chair and the other on the floor, ready to get going. The Menezes are a great family. Not only did John work hard, but his wife was just as hardworking as Dorothy. They are great, honest people.

I met a lot of nice people on the golf course. I loved Hollister and started to play most of my golf there and in Monterey at Ridgemark Golf and Country Club. At Ridgemark, there were some guys from San Jose who played there. I got acquainted with them and made a lot of money betting on the game. What I did when I played with them was to put a Band-Aid around the head of my driver shaft. You wouldn't believe how many people worried about the head of my driver flying off. It was the perfect distraction!

When you're playing sports or poker, you use "tools," as the professionals call them. Most people who play for big money get nervous and can't play. But there are some people who love competition and don't get nervous. I always loved competition, and so did my son.

I had a friend named Willis Evans and I used to win bets on golf games against him. One time, he came to Turlock looking for me. I was out working, as usual. When I got back, they said he was upstairs waiting for me.

I wasn't really scared of him, because he invited me to Monterey to play for money. I only bet a little just to see how he played.

He didn't win anything. You see, when he played, all he did was complain about his clothes through the first nine holes. I realized he was easy when all he did was complain about everything.

Whenever he needed money, he would haul olive trees to Palm Springs and sell them there, so Dorothy and I would go to Santa Nella outside Los Banos to give him money to buy gas for his truck. But every time Willis got paid, he would find some way to lose it.

One time, I went with him to Palm Springs, and he introduced me to John Templeton, the man who bought his olive trees. John had built the Palm Desert Golf Course. Boy, I sure did learn a lot from him about business, and in return I gave him golf lessons. He was a very wealthy man, but he had a reputation for never betting any money on golf, so I never asked him to bet with me. Willis sometimes asked John to bet, but it just made him mad.

When Willis had some money, he would buy everyone drinks and tip the waitresses.

Willis was the one who talked me into going to Phoenix, Arizona, to try out for the Senior Golf Tournament. He paid my way and wanted to caddy for me, but I missed the alternate spot by three shots.

I could tell a lot of stories about Willis. He was raised in Watsonville and said he came from a very poor family, like I did. He used to tell me he slept under a fruit tree when he was growing up. But when he had money, he sure did have a big heart.

Willis died at the age of 58. I didn't find out until after he had passed away. He was cremated and his ashes spread over the golf course in Santa Cruz. There were times I felt like I could have knocked him in the head. But down deep, he did have a good heart, and those waitresses really liked him because he was a big tipper.

Chapter 15

Family and Business

I often think about the way I grew up and how we survived. It's so different compared to today.

The best way is that everything should start with the family, and the parents should let children know who is boss, without being mean about it. It is important to discipline kids when they are wrong.

What really gets me is people saying, "I can't make my kids behave." That's because they don't really care about them. People love to have kids, but they don't know how to discipline them. Don't blame the kids, it's no one else's fault except your own.

We raised our kids with strict order, but we always complimented them when they did a good job. But if the job wasn't done right, Dorothy and I would go over it with them and correct what needed to be done. After they did it right, we would brag about what a good job they did.

When you go watch your kids perform in sports, just keep quiet so they don't get too nervous to play. Hard practice — just like hard work — will accomplish a lot, and they will have fun at the same time.

Watch what your kids like to do and really brag on them, whether you like it or not, as long as it's not something that's bad. Stay with them all the way and build them up.

It is good to get the kids involved with businesses the parents are working at. If our kids didn't like what we asked them to do, my wife would put them in some other job that they liked better. Help your kids find the type of work they love.

It was great that my wife, kids and I all worked together as a team and as a family. If Dorothy and I came home late from working all day, the kids were cooking dinner. If we got home before they did, we would cook. It's hard to believe how well they could cook. Even if it wasn't perfect, I would always brag on them. But I didn't have to lie — they were good cooks! Then when we sat down for supper, we had the best conversations about what we did that day.

I admit that I don't know everything about raising a family. But if you take your kids and show them how to work, if you brag on them when they do something well, if you compliment them when they do their chores, if you see that they abide by the rules of your home, you will be very proud of them, and of yourself.

Having sensible rules at home makes it easier for everyone in the family.

I hope this book will help young people appreciate their mothers and fathers. I encourage children to help their parents whenever they can, at home and in business. A family that works and plays together will stay together — don't ever forget it. Our family did those things and we did well together.

If I didn't have my wife and kids, I would never have made it. They came up with good ideas, and I would pay attention! Most fathers think they know everything, but Dorothy and the kids had good ideas, too.

In the end, I would never have had all those businesses if it weren't for my family being there. They helped me more than you can imagine.

I used to hear people say, "I had to work hard and I don't want my kids to have to work that hard," or "I don't want my kids to have to work at all."

But if you don't teach your kids to work hard, they will grow up to be lazy bums, and you can't blame anyone but yourself. I think it's a good thing to be raised to work hard. All my kids were business people, even when they were still in school.

Our daughter Kim was only in the sixth grade, but she was very sharp at running the cash register at our steak house and Mexican restaurant, which were next to our pizza parlor in the Herb Lowe shopping center on

Highway 152 in Los Banos. Our manager, Peggy Brown, put in a taller chair so Kim could sit and take the money as she ran the register. Peggy and I would get a kick out of watching the people through the window when they left, counting their money to see if Kim had given them the right change. She could run the register better than most people. She was very sharp, even in grade school.

In addition to my family, I had some great people helping me run the restaurant. But you wouldn't believe how our kids took over the businesses where they were working.

Once your kids learn something, they can do as good a job as you. When my kids told me, "Dad, get out of here," I knew what to do. I would go over to the side and watch them, and they did great! Then I would brag on them. You wouldn't believe how many tips they made, which made them do even better!

In Los Banos at the corner of Sixth and I streets, the entire block was vacant except for Eddie's restaurant. We leased the whole block with options to buy. I remodeled the buildings and leased out all except one building, which was our children's store.

Dorothy named the store Junior Junction. She and Darla designed the store, and it turned out beautifully. Darla learned how to run those stores. I would drive Darla and Dorothy to the clothing market in San Francisco to buy their stock of children's clothes while I sat in the hallway to wait for them. I was their chauffeur. They

A while later, a friend of mine, Steve Rodriguez, wanted me to run a gravel business in town, so we took one over. The owners decided they wanted it back, so we gave it back after they agreed to take back the note that we had assumed from them.

I told Steve, "Just get a couple of trucks and start your own business." So he started his own trucking business and has done real well.

I was talking to a good friend of mine who had decided to close his dairy because he was losing money. He said, "You know, Darrell, I remember your handshake was better than most people's word."

I told him that when someone came to do business with me, and I saw them in their suits, ties and with a briefcase, I thought they were rich. But I was influenced by the way they looked. Other guys who go everywhere wearing old clothes look like they don't have anything, but you would be surprised what they have and how honest they are. Don't get me wrong, they are clean, not dirty. They just like to wear old clothes.

If people today worked as hard as we did back then, there wouldn't be as much unemployment and welfare. I don't have a lot of respect for men who get laid off on purpose three months out of the year so they can go down to the coffee shop and shoot the breeze.

My advice is that you can become successful by doing the things you like to do. Always look for something you love and make it your work. That way, you will love to go to work and you will be successful at it.

For young people just starting in life, and even while you're still in school, I think you should find something you love to do every day, even something like a trade. Then, when you have to go to work, you will love what you are doing. If you hate your work, it will make you miserable the rest of your life. So if you love to drive a truck, then learn to drive a truck to the very best of your ability.

But even if you find out you don't like it once you've tried it, you can sell the business to someone who might like it. Make sure you get up front whatever you have invested in the business and then you can finance the rest until they pay you in full.

If you love what you do, you can make it work. A lot of people I played golf with would say they hate to go to work every day. I say, if you find you don't love what you do, love it until you can get rid of it, and make some money getting rid of it.

A lot of people will buy a business without realizing how much work is involved running it — sometimes it's a 24-hour-a-day job, not an eight-hour-a-day job.

Too often, people buy a business from you, and when you try to stay and help them, they think they know everything and tell you to go away. Soon they realize they didn't know it all. I usually stayed with a business for about a month to see how they liked it.

If you ever buy a business, it will save you a lot of headaches and a lot of money if you get the previous owner's advice. It's best to go through a bulk transfer sale or a lawyer. If you don't, you could be liable for their debts. That's very important.

And if you sell a business, don't let them take it until they put the money down with a lawyer or the bulk transfer sale. Better to sell it and get your money up front, because if they ruin the business, they may try to give it back to you without having paid you anything. That way, if they want to walk, you will make a bunch of money and still have the business. It's fair to look after yourself as long as you do it honestly.

A good rule to remember is that if something is wrong in the business, don't buy it. But in sports or cards, you win any way you can. It's called hustling. And I will admit I was a hustler. It was the one way I made money in Newman when things were tough.

Remember that three-hour time difference between the east and west? A lot of people never figured out that I always knew ahead of time who won a fight. I took advantage of it, but I believe that if they knew my trick, they would have done the same thing to me. But be careful, because gambling can be like drugs or anything that becomes habit-forming.

One golfer named John who was married four or five times lost more than fifty million dollars in Las Vegas. He is broke today. I know a lot of other people who are broke from gambling. The only way most of them stopped was to go broke. There's an old saying: "Gambling money has no home."

When it comes to success, I really believe that when you don't think about things you want to accomplish and instead think of ways to keep from working, you really don't want to succeed. One thing that makes me sad about our great country is that most people seem to be looking for a way to keep from working.

When you hear people saying mean things about their friends because they are successful, it is usually because they are too lazy to work. And I'm not talking about working just eight hours a day. When you own your own business, the time to sleep is when you get the work done. How would you like to go three days without getting into bed to sleep? I have done that. I would take hot showers and go work some more. I thought it was fun, and I was successful.

Too many people worry about the eight hours they have to work, but if you love what you do, you never worry about the time. A word of advice, if you work for someone else as your boss, make sure you work hard for him, because he is the one who makes a living for you.

Many people are jealous of their boss, but they seem to forget that he is the one who pays them. If he goes out of business, they lose their job.

The number one thing you need to do is be honest and work hard, and you will be successful. Sometimes your friends will be jealous of you, but that is human nature.

Be Successful

No matter how bad your life is, you can do great if you think positive all the time. No matter what happens, stay strong, work hard and be honest. As the years go by, you will be successful in your work and business.

I have seen many people who do real well, then when things start going bad, they get crooked. You always lose when you do that.

I know people who let their kids break them after they worked all their lives for retirement. They trust them, and lose everything.

Before doing anything like this, find someone, such as an attorney, to advise you.

Here's an example: I talked to a 70-year-old friend who works at Walmart and asked him, "What are you doing working here?"

He told me his story. He co-signed for his kids on their home, now he could lose his home and he has payments again. And do you think they care? No. That's why you have to be careful. I know you love your kids, but you could lose everything.

Some people have certain natural talent that God gives them. I have worked very hard during my life in the barbering and beauty business, so I know what I am talking about.

Today, some barbers just skin the customer's head and they think they've got something. I have seen people on television who have paid a lot of money for a haircut. But it's not just about cutting hair, you have to shape their hair to suit the shape of their head and face. It's true for women, too.

I can remember people coming into our business who seemed mad at the whole world, but we treated them so nice that they became some of the best customers I ever had. But I would never let them treat my employees or my family mean. If they did, I would personally run them off.

One time, there was a Christmas party at our steak house for the employees of a local bank, and our manager was serving the table. One of the men kept trying to put his hands on her. I went out there with her and tried to get him to come into the kitchen so I could talk to him. He wouldn't come, so I told him what I thought of him right there at the table. His manager didn't believe me so I told him to leave. Other people who were in the restaurant came up and told me that they would vouch for me if it went to court. There was even a lawyer there who said he would represent me. It never went that far.

Some of those that I did run off would eventually come back, apologize, and become good customers.

Let me share with you something that is worth a million dollars to your business: Giving service to your customer is very important. I've seen some people who never gave good service, and they went broke and wondered why.

When your customers come in, give them a big smile and say, "Hello, how are you doing today?" Also be polite when they leave. It doesn't hurt to run to the door and thank them for their business. There are two things I always did in the businesses I owned: I always remembered to greet them, and I also said, "Thank you very much." So that goes to show you, if you want to be successful, you can. Just be honest and work hard.

When I built my golf driving range in the Merced and Atwater area, you wouldn't believe how many golf tips we gave to people. It was good for business. We also had great stereo music playing on our deck where people could sit, listen to music and watch the people hit golf balls. I tuned our radio to Merced's KABX Oldies 97.5 radio station — we loved their music.

All the people who worked at the driving range were taught to treat everyone nicely, and that is why we did so well. All the people in town treated us the same way in return.

I have met a lot of people in my time, and I've seen that most of them get into things they know nothing about. I have seen people go broke in the housing industry because they don't know what they're doing, or they pay too much for their land to start with and they over-build. That is called greed. It not only happens to builders, but also large landowners, like farmers and cattle ranchers who went broke because they got themselves over-extended and couldn't get the money to pay their debts.

When you own a business, you have to stay very involved. I have seen some people build their business up and then they think they can be gone all the time. They wonder why they're not making any money and why they're going broke. It's because they aren't there to watch their business and interact with the customers.

My friend had a Western Auto store, and this is how he lost his business. He was always playing golf or gin rummy and wasn't at the store. Not only did he lose his business, he lost his wife and family.

Some people just don't realize what they have. When I lived in Wyco holler, the only businesses there were the coal mine, store and beer joint, and they were all owned by the company that owned the mine.

When I was just a little boy watching Mrs. Flaim cutting hair with hand clippers, I decided that cutting hair was what I wanted to do with my life. Even at such a young age, I wanted to be a barber, and that is what I became. I loved every day I worked as a barber. Many times I never even stopped for lunch or a glass of water until I got off work — that is how much I loved barbering and the competition with other barbers.

Owning my own business was one of the best things I ever did.

Chapter 16

Dorothy Passes Away

Dorothy passed away from cancer in the early 1980s, at the age of 41. About a year or so after our move to Los Banos, she got cancer and only lived four months after her diagnosis. She was gone so fast I couldn't believe it.

She was a good Christian woman, and everybody loved her. She was a great lady and a wonderful mother.

Dorothy was also a very good businesswoman and a hard worker. She was a great real estate salesperson. The broker I worked with, Scotty Henderson, used to kid me about her selling more than I did. She was always good at whatever she did.

Besides loving to sell real estate, we enjoyed being together and had a lot of fun. She was such a wonderful dancer that I loved to dance with her when we went out.

I also taught her how to play golf. Her very first year as a golfer, we played in a husband-and-wife tournament and finished second. She was a great competitor in everything she did, and I was very proud of her.

If my wife hadn't died so young, there is no telling what kind of businesses we would have bought. I believe we would have bought more property together.

After I lost Dorothy, I slowed down on buying and building businesses because that took a lot of time and energy. I didn't have the drive for building businesses like I did before she passed.

So instead, I got rid of most of our businesses. I didn't need them, and our kids wanted to do other things. I continued to sell real estate and I opened my own office, Westside Real Estate.

Sometimes I would sit in the real estate office conference room dressed in my donut shop work clothes, counting my money from donut sales. When one woman saw all that cash, she told me that if I ever wanted to sell the shop, I should talk to her first. When I decided to sell the donut shop, I did talk to her and her husband, and they bought it. They saw what I made each day, and they wanted it, so I sold it.

The one thing Dorothy used to tell me was, "If I die before you, don't come to the grave to visit me because I will be in heaven," and I always believed that. So I don't worry about her, bless her heart.

I thank God she left me three great kids, but it still wasn't the same after she was gone. The reason my kids are so great is because they had a wonderful mother.

People don't realize what a shock it is to the kids when a family loses their wife and mother when she's 41 years old. The only thing I wished was that it would have been me who died instead of their mother. They were very close to her. I think children are usually closer to their mother than their father.

Always treat your wife and mother of your children well and appreciate her; you don't know how long you are going to have her.

Everybody who met her, liked her. She never acted like she was better than anyone else.

I could write forever about her. The worst words I ever heard in my life were when the doctor told me she only had four months to live.

Be Careful in Business

Living in Los Banos right after Dorothy died, I was standing in the kitchen one Monday morning, staring out the window. I decided to go to Hollister and play golf and look around some.

Hollister is a great town. The National Weather Bureau says it has the best weather in the United States, and I believe them.

As I looked around, I started thinking about opening a Century 21 real estate office there. At that time, they didn't have one.

I was going to go into partnership with another guy, so I met with him in Hollister. When I read the contract he had drawn up, I realized it was all in his favor. He didn't write the contract in a way that would be fair to both of us, so I handed the papers back to him without signing and walked away.

You see, what happens a lot of time is if you don't understand your contract, you need to take it to someone who does understand it, like a real estate attorney, so you don't get cheated.

Chapter 17

Sherma

After Dorothy died, I was single for about eleven years. I kept myself busy working and playing golf.

Then in 1991, I met and married my present wife, Sherma, a great Christian lady.

She used to come over to the high school field where I hit golf balls, and I would take her golfing with me.

We started dating quietly, and then one day she said, "Darrell, let's go to Reno and get married." So we went. It was just the two of us — none of our family was with us.

When we got back from Reno, I asked her if she wanted to live in her house or mine. We decided to move into my house.

I love my wife very much, and we get along well. One thing we don't believe in is fighting and arguing. We get along fine and work well together, like I did for so long with Dorothy.

I continued working in real estate until Sherma and I built the Santa Fe Golf Driving Range in the Merced and Atwater area. It was one of the best things I ever did, besides barbering.

We found the land, and from 1992 to 1993, we built the driving range on about 22 acres on Santa Fe Road.

I designed it myself, and it was beautiful!

We had 72 hitting areas, plus a putting green and a large clubhouse. I worked in the clubhouse, built golf clubs, and gave golf lessons. Sherma helped with the bookkeeping and also worked in the clubhouse. She was very good with the customers and was a big help in the business. We did real well there.

I had the best neighbors at the golf range, Harvey Freitas and his son Kevin. They did all of my outside grounds work. They sure taught me a lot about the ground and grass, like when to turn the sprinklers on to keep everything green.

You wouldn't believe all the fun we had. The people of Merced, Atwater and other small towns in the area were very supportive.

School golf teams would come and practice for their golf matches. I even had four schools at one time practicing in private hitting areas. They were very respectful to us, and nobody bothered them.

If I hadn't been living 45 miles away in Los Banos at the time, I don't think I would have sold it.

If you ever want to play golf, don't beat your brains out. Take some lessons. That's more important than buying fancy clubs. Lessons first, then clubs — and a lot of practice!

As long as you can walk, you can play. But when you get old, you aren't going to hit it very far. But it's fun, and it's better than doing nothing. Find some kind of sport after you retire, maybe even go to a driving range and practice all the fundamentals.

Even if you don't play golf seriously, your kids might love it and want to enter tournaments. Remember, don't yell at your kids, just watch them play and brag on them.

We had the driving range fifteen years. As I got older, I thought we'd better sell it, because if something were to happen to me, my wife couldn't do all that work.

Even though we sold it, Sherma and I still try and work together on projects that come along. There are a lot of women who are smarter then men and we should listen to them.

I try to help my wife and take care of her, making sure she is feeling well and that she has a good church to go to. We try not to fight or argue because I had enough of that up in the holler.

After selling the driving range, I went back in the real estate business, working on some commercial ventures. I am also getting ready to patent a project and if I am successful, you may see it on TV.

And, of course, I am still playing golf.

Part 6

LOOKING BACK

Chapter 18

Wilcox Family — Later Years

The best thing my mother ever did was buy 28 acres (two lots) in Damascus, Virginia, and get all the kids out of that holler. She used the $10,000 she got when my brother Joe got killed in the war. The property is still in the family.

All of my brothers and sisters got good jobs and did really well.

My mother and father both died in Damascus, Virginia.

My father died when he was coming home from town and he had to cross a bridge that went to his house. The river was up, and he fell in and drowned. They found him by the bridge the next day.

My mother died years later from a heart condition.

It's terrible to admit that I went to my mother's funeral but not my father's. If you knew what I went through with him, you wouldn't have, either. I hope he is in heaven. I love him, even if he was mean.

If anyone was my hero, it was my mother. When I went back to her funeral, the last words I said to her were, "Mom, I am glad I never caused you any trouble." I was so proud I got my high school diploma for her.

Always remember, if you have a great mom and dad, put your arms around them and tell them you love them. You need to remember they're always behind you — when everybody else lets you down, your mom and dad are always there.

My oldest sister, Vivian, was the third child in our family. She used to help my mother doing chores in the house. Dad would never let her date, so she slipped off and got married to a man who was an ex-con. They moved to Baltimore and had two boys. One of her boys was murdered in a park. She had a tough life and finally left her husband. She still lives in Baltimore. Thank God, she didn't go back to the holler.

My brother Robert passed away in 2010, at the age of 87. Robert was a really handsome guy. He had a girlfriend, Renee, who waited for him though World War II. She worked as a secretary at the coal camp and was one of the nicest and prettiest women I ever saw.

After Robert got out of the service, Renee waited seven more years for him. But he never asked her to marry him, so she married another man. She used to tell my sister that she never loved her husband as well as she loved Robert.

It's hard to say why Robert never married her or anyone else. I never understood it. Maybe he needed to help our family more than he wanted to get married. He lived at home and was a huge help to mom. The money he gave us made a big difference.

You know how people go on vacations to different parts of the country? They should go back into those hills in West Virginia and they would be surprised to see how they live. They are used to it because they have always lived that way. That is how they were raised, and they don't know any different.

I remember when my brother Harold and a friend came out to visit me in California and play golf. It didn't matter all the things he saw and experienced here, he couldn't wait to get back to West Virginia. That was his home. Summer, winter, fall and spring — no matter what the season was, he was used to it.

I would like to say something about my brothers and sisters. They might not have graduated, but they were good businesspeople — hardworking and self-made. Harold even became a barber, like I did. We had nothing handed to us. That goes to show you, you can be successful if you're honest and work hard.

Chapter 19

A Good Life

I think in all of my ventures and adventures I liked being a barber more than anything else. But if I hadn't had my wife and children, I could never have done all the things I did.

It is very important to remember that our kids are watching us all the time, so we need to make a good impression on them. I know, sometimes we forget and make a mistake.

As children, we were taught to respect our parents and elders. It's different now, with kids doing what they want to do. If I wasn't so old, I would love to work with a program to help kids and their families.

Young people today should be thankful that they live at this time, in this century, and in the greatest country in the world.

Growing up, we made what we had and lived the way we did because we didn't know any better.

Up in the holler we had an old saying, "We were poor, but we just didn't know it." All the folks who lived in the West Virginia holler were poor, but we thought everyone in the world lived the same way.

I remember when my folks finally bought a refrigerator with the motor on the top — boy, did we think that was something.

It is hard for me to believe that our family didn't even own a car, yet today you drive by a school and all the kids drive better cars than I do. If folks from back in the holler could see what kids drive to school these days, they would never believe it. Some parents don't even make their kids work for their cars. Kids today don't know how lucky they are to live in the United States of America. There is no country in the world as good as ours.

When I look back, I can't believe we lived like that. I thank God that he protected us.

All I can say is we survived the holler, and I'm glad I went into the service and got to leave there when I was stationed in San Diego.

It makes me feel good knowing all the positive things that happened to me after I left Wyco holler. Even when I went back to Virginia for my mom's funeral, it was still the same there — nothing to do. I was glad to get back home to California, where we are blessed to have many opportunities and things to do.

The people in West Virginia are good, nice people, and it's home to them. But I don't think I will ever go back again, because California is my home now.

Today, almost all the houses in the holler are gone, and the mine closed down in the 1970s or '80s. There's no store or beer joint, just the old church building and a post office left for a few people who still live up there.

People are trying to modernize the holler now. I'm glad, because we need them to preserve the history of how we were raised.

I've lived in the east and the west, and I'm convinced that there is no other country as good as the United States of America! It's the one place in the world where you can make it simply by believing in yourself, working hard and being honest.

THE END

PHOTO CREDITS

Main Cover Photo: This is where the Slab Fork joins the Guyandotte River in Mullens, photo by Tim Kiser.

Back Cover Photo: Darrell and Sherma Wilcox, 2011, photo by Annette Williams.

Pg. 105: Walter "Red" Wilcox, and Carrie (Gillen) Wilcox, photos courtesy of Darrell Wilcox.

Pg. 107: Darrell's father, Walter, as a child. Walter's father, also named Walter, is one of the men pictured, but which one is unknown. Photos courtesy of Darrell Wilcox and Johnny Wilcox.

Pg. 109: Darrell Wilcox's original birth certificate, photo courtesy of Darrell Wilcox.

Pg. 111: The bridge where Darrell broke his arm while sledding, and the Wilcox house, photos courtesy of Darrell Wilcox.

Pg. 113: Miners of Wyco Coal Company, photos courtesy of Darrell Wilcox.

Pg. 115: Dr. Wilkinson and family, and Dr. Wilkinson's home, photos courtesy of Darrell Wilkinson Jr.

Pg. 117: Wyco mine superintendent's home, and Wyco Church, photos courtesy of Darrell Wilkinson Jr.

Pg. 119: Wyco black families' church, and Wyco boarding house, photos courtesy of Johnny Wilcox.

Pg. 121: Wyco Grade School, photo courtesy of Darrell Wilkinson Jr. Darrell Wilcox's reading certificate, photo courtesy of Darrell Wilcox.

Pg. 123: Wyco general store, photo courtesy of Darrell Wilcox. Mullens High School, photo courtesy of Coach Lewis D'Antoni.

Pg. 125: Mullens, West Virginia. Top photo courtesy of City of Mullens. Bottom photo courtesy of Darrell Wilcox.

Pg. 127: Barber college diploma, and U.S. Naval Training Center appointment certificate, photos courtesy of Darrell Wilcox.

Pg. 129: U.S. Naval Training Center, San Diego (Darrell is in back row, second from left), and Darrell's Navy portrait, photos courtesy of Darrell Wilcox.

Pg. 131: USS Kearsarge, official U.S. Navy photograph. Darrell's Navy days, photo courtesy of Darrell Wilcox.

Pg. 133: In the Navy, photos courtesy of Darrell Wilcox.

Pg. 135: Barber shop on the USS Kearsarge, photo courtesy of Darrell Wilcox.

Pg. 137: Darrell and Dorothy Wilcox, photos courtesy of Kim Miranda.

Pg. 139: The Wilcox family, photos courtesy of Kim Miranda.

Pg. 141: Golf tournaments, photos courtesy of Darrell Wilcox.

Pg. 143: Official barber identification photo, and Santa Fe Golf Driving Range, photos courtesy of Darrell Wilcox.

Pg. 145: Darrell and Sherma Wilcox, photos by Annette Williams.

INDEX

260

Made in the USA
Lexington, KY
12 January 2013